FRIENDSHIP
at the
MARGINS

Discovering Mutuality in Service and Mission

CHRISTOPHER L. HEUERTZ
& CHRISTINE D. POHL

Resources for Reconciliation

series editors

EMMANUEL KATONGOLE & CHRIS RICE

IVP Books

An imprint of InterVarsity Press
Downers Grove, Illinois

InterVarsity Press
P.O. Box 1400, Downers Grove, IL 60515-1426
World Wide Web: www.ivpress.com
E-mail: email@ivpress.com

InterVarsity Press® is the book-publishing division of InterVarsity Christian Fellowship/USA®, a student movement active on campus at hundreds of universities, colleges and schools of nursing in the United States of America, and a member movement of the International Fellowship of Evangelical Students. For information about local and regional activities, write Public Relations Dept., InterVarsity Christian Fellowship/USA, 6400 Schroeder Rd., P.O. Box 7895, Madison, WI 53707-7895, or visit the IVCF website at <www.intervarsity.org>.

Scripture quotations, unless otherwise noted, are from the New Revised Standard Version of the Bible, copyright 1989 by the Division of Christian Education of the National Council of the Churches of Christ in the USA. Used by permission. All rights reserved.

While all of the stories in this book are true, some of the names and identifying details have been changed to protect the privacy of those involved.

Study guide written by Sarah Jobe.

Design: Rebecca Larson

Images: Jesus Eats with Friends © 2009 Rick Beerhorst/Eyekons www.eyekons.com

ISBN 978-0-8308-3454-9

Printed in the United States of America ∞

Library of Congress Cataloging-in-Publication Data

Heuertz, Christopher L., 1971-
  Friendship at the margins: discovering mutuality in service and
mission / Christopher L. Heuertz, Christine D. Pohl.
     p. cm.—(Resources for reconciliation)
  Includes bibliographical references (p.   ).
  ISBN 978-0-8308-3454-9 (pbk.: alk. paper)
    1. Church work with the poor. 2. Word Made Flesh (Organization) 3.
Friendship—Religious aspects—Christianity. I. Pohl, Christine D.
II. Title.
  BV639.P6H58 2010
  261.8'325—dc22
                                                                2009048954

P 25 24 23 22 21 20 19 18 17 16 15 14 13 12 11 10 9 8 7 6 5 4 3 2 1

Y 31 30 29 28 27 26 25 24 23 22 21 20 19 18 17 16 15 14 13 12 11 10

"In a world of aggressive economics, cynical politics and excessive ideological certitude, everyone is an adversary. Such aggression, cynicism and certitude, moreover, produce unbearable alienation. Here Heuertz and Pohl offer a quiet, honest probe of generous friendship as an antidote to the great social pathology that devours us. With narrative particularity and acute neighborly sensibility, they witness to the cost and risk of friendship, which at its best cannot be done wholesale. This account concerns the truth of human life made fleshly—immediate, face-to-face, dangerous and transformative. They offer much to ponder about how, in a world of too many adversaries, the practice of friendship among the weak and unnoticed may be our hope for the future. A tall order, likely our only alternative!"
WALTER BRUEGGEMANN, Columbia Theological Seminary

"*Friendship at the Margins* is not only an insight into the world of community but penned words that will inspire and challenge everything we know on the subject. This insightful book is not something that I am going to skim through, but a mirror to reflect upon from time to time for the rest of my life."
STEPHEN CHRISTIAN, cofounder, Faceless International, and singer, Anberlin/Anchor & Braille

"*Friendship at the Margins* calls for a radical reorientation from thinking about 'causes' to thinking about people. We don't just want to help 'the poor,' we want to help Sujana, Madu and Adalina. And in helping and serving, we discover how much we receive from relationships that stretch beyond our normal social circles. I could not more strongly recommend this book to anyone who wants to make a difference in our world."
PETER GREER, president, HOPE International, and coauthor of *The Poor Will Be Glad*

"*Friendship at the Margins* shares learning from following the path of Jesus and Paul of befriending people at the margins of 'respectable' society today. This is no ivory tower theology but theology worked out in the bittersweet experience of becoming friends with those we respectable people call the 'poor.' There is much here to inspire those of us who think of mission in terms of both telling and serving. In fact I would go further and say that this book is about the essence of Christian mission."
DEWI HUGHES, theological advisor, Tearfund

"A must-read book. Most think ministry to the poor and least of these means 'reaching out' and then walking away. But *Friendship at the Margins* defines ministry to the poor as the gift of friendship and building the bridge of hospitality by living among them and with them. I highly recommend you not only read this book, but get involved and learn more about the incredible work of Word Made Flesh."
BRAD LOMENICK, director, Catalyst

"*Friendship at the Margins* brings the simple concept of friendship and adds a nuance that challenges current mission models. Its stories bring clarity to the difficulties brought on by relationships with people in precarious situations. But it ultimately paints a startling picture of sustained journeying with Jesus. A thoughtful and inspiring read."
NIKKI TOYAMA-SZETO, program director, Urbana, and coeditor of *More Than Serving Tea*

"*Friendship at the Margins* weaves together masterfully the life of contemplative activists, friendships, spirituality, simplicity and community to create a refreshingly demystified understanding of mission. The book deals with some 'pain points' in Christian missions like career, community and popular approaches which have become the order of the day in the mission field, unfortunately. The book presents friendship not merely as a manipulative method, but as the heart of mission itself. The authors through the book provide rich insights into their passion and experience."
JAYAKUMAR CHRISTIAN, national director, World Vision India

"The loud may get the most attention, but more often than not it's the gentle, humble and highly relational that will change the world. Chris Heuertz is one of those people—listen carefully, he has much to say!"
MARGARET FEINBERG (www.margaretfeinberg.com), author of *The Organic God* and *Scouting the Divine*

"*Friendship at the Margins* is an important book arising at a time when our culture values success and objects more than relationships. This book is an important challenge that theology must be both received and lived and that our faith requires the ongoing struggle and joy of what may be at times difficult friendships. Calling for substance over form in our actions of justice, Chris Heuertz and Christine Pohl remind us that the living out of God's justice is a two-way street of giving and receiving."
SOONG-CHAN RAH, Milton B. Engebretson Associate Professor of Church Growth and Evangelism, North Park Theological Seminary, and author of *The Next Evangelicalism*

"Without question you will be challenged and inspired by the words written in *Friendship at the Margins*. The words, insights and challenge put forth by Chris and Christine will help each one of us truly experience what it means to be a follower of Jesus."
MIKE FOSTER, senior creative principal, PlainJoe Studios, and cofounder, People of the Second Chance and XXXchurch.com

"Don't miss this book! Heuertz and Pohl extend a gracious invitation to all those of us who thirst for life that really is life. *Friendship at the Margins* welcomes readers to participate in kingdom friendships which refresh the hearts of all who will drink deeply. Expect to be nourished, challenged and transformed by this book."
MARGOT STARBUCK, author of *The Girl in the Orange Dress*

Contents

Series Preface

The Resources for Reconciliation Book Series

A partnership between InterVarsity Press and the Center for Reconciliation at Duke Divinity School, Resources for Reconciliation books address what it means to pursue hope in areas of brokenness, including the family, the city, the poor, the disabled, Christianity and Islam, racial and ethnic divisions, violent conflicts, and the environment. The series seeks to offer a fresh and distinctive vision for reconciliation as God's mission and a journey toward God's new creation in Christ. Each book is authored by two leading voices, one in the field of practice or grassroots experience, the other from the academy. Each book is grounded in the biblical story, engages stories and places of pain and hope, and seeks to help readers to live faithfully—a rich mix of theology, context and practice.

This book series was born out of the mission of the Duke Divinity School Center for Reconciliation: *Advancing God's mission of reconciliation in a divided world by cultivating new leaders, communicating wisdom and hope, and connecting in outreach to strengthen leadership.* A divided world needs people with the vision, spiritual maturity and daily skills integral to the journey of reconciliation. The church needs fresh resources—a mix of biblical vision, social skills of social and historical analysis, and practical gifts of spirituality and social leadership—in order to pursue reconciliation in real places, from congregations to communities.

The ministry of reconciliation is not reserved for experts. It is the core of God's mission and an everyday call of the Christian life. These books are written to equip and stimulate God's people to be more faithful ambassadors of reconciliation in a fractured world.

For more information, email the Duke Divinity School Center for Reconciliation at reconciliation@div.duke.edu, or visit our website: <www.divinity.duke.edu/reconciliation>.

Emmanuel Katongole
Chris Rice
Center codirectors and series editors

Introduction

*"Go . . . and make disciples of all nations, baptizing them
in the name of the Father and of the Son and of the Holy Spirit,
and teaching them to obey everything that I have commanded you."*

Matthew 28:19-20

*J*esus' parting words to his followers ignited a missionary movement that has now spanned millennia. In his teaching, he left no
doubt that every commandment and every undertaking should de-
rive from—and point to—love for God and neighbor. But under-
girding everything Jesus said and did is God's love for each person,
most clearly evident in the love and sacrifice of Jesus himself.

Jesus made our outreach, mission and ministry very personal
when he said in Matthew 25 that when we have responded to the
needs of the least of his brothers or sisters, we've responded to

him. When we've fed or clothed, sheltered or visited a person in need, Jesus has experienced our expressions of care as ministry to himself.

Sacrificial love is at the heart of mission and reconciliation. But love and reconciliation can seem pretty abstract until we ask questions like *What does reconciliation look like when you love Jesus and want the best for people who are caught in situations of terrible evil, need or despair? How would our lives and our ministries be different if our understandings of love emphasized friendship?*

This little book is an extended reflection on these questions. It contains many stories of friendship and love and puts friendship at the center of reflection on reconciliation and mission. We want to ask *What difference does it make for mission, discipleship and the church when friendship with people who are poor is a central dimension of our lives? What is the impact on those with whom we minister? How are we changed? What does it mean for the church, for reconciliation and for the practice of mission?*

Friendships are revelatory of truth. Within friendship we learn truths about the other person we couldn't know any other way except through a context of trust and fidelity. Within friendship we learn about ourselves as we see our love and action through the eyes of another who loves and trusts us. And relationships forged among friends can open into deeper understandings of God's love and concerns.

Evangelism, and even the notion of mission itself, has sometimes been reduced to the words we share with another person, telling them about Jesus, salvation or eternal life. Words are important, but they can also be cheap. If we use words and get words in response, sometimes we think we've done mission or evangelism. Ministry among poor and vulnerable people reminds us that words are rarely enough—what each of us needs is to know that we are loved by Jesus, beloved of God. Everything else flows from that. In situations of injustice or despair, words alone are particularly insufficient. People need to be loved and valued by others. They need to see what love looks like.

THE GIFT OF FRIENDSHIP

Much of this book is drawn from experiences of friendship in hard places and from reflection on what those friendships mean for the church. Looking closely at particular stories and engaging actual experience allow us to tease out insights and challenges.

Many of the stories come from one community in particular, a community that has chosen to minister in some of the most difficult places among some of the most poor, vulnerable and violated people in the world. Numbering around two hundred people in the formal embrace of the organization, Word Made Flesh has formed small communities that attempt to take Jesus' incarnation seriously— his willingness to become flesh and "move into the neighborhood" (John 1:14 *The Message*).

Word Made Flesh (WMF) describes itself as a community of contemplative activists who follow the most vulnerable of the world's poor to God's heart. Their call is to practice the presence and proclamation of the kingdom of God among friends who are poor by embodying love and holding onto hope. Situating their efforts in a Christian faith that bears witness to hope, they attempt to live out the character of a good God in a world that has many reasons to question the possibility of God's goodness.

Over the years, WMF teams have established drop-in centers, children's homes, hospices, community centers and advocacy programs in India, Nepal, Thailand, Romania, Moldova, Sierra Leone, Peru, Bolivia, Brazil and Argentina. Staff members live and work among populations of kids who live and work on the streets, who are former child soldiers or victims of human trafficking. Relationships are central to WMF, shaping when and where the communities are started and how the communities and ministries are led. Decision-making processes are as decentralized as possible so that the participation of friends who are poor is at the heart of the community.

Helping people recover their dignity and the possibility of a good future, and helping the WMF community embrace fuller understandings of friendship, involves avoiding language and practices that contribute to the reduction of some friends to an over-generalized notion of "the poor." By trying not to over-identify people with their difficult contexts and by calling friends by their actual names when possible, WMF communities offer the hope that comes with affirming the distinctive and divine imprint of God in each person.

For WMF staff members, friendships forged with children and women who have been exploited open windows into realities that are worse than nightmares. Learning to negotiate power dynamics within relationships between people who are extremely vulnerable and those with more conventional resources creates opportunities to explore complicated ethical tensions. Having friends who are poor at the center of a community's life, rhythms and purpose offers glimpses into what reconciliation with the so-called other actually looks like.

When small groups of WMF staff have located themselves in hard places—in places marked by tremendous suffering and abject poverty—people who were very, very poor sought them out. They came, not so much as seekers, but as neighbors looking to be friends. They invited the WMF folks to their homes for a meal or for tea. Though unable to communicate in words in the early days, they'd open a photo album and try to break down the walls of language by sharing parts of their own stories.

In the midst of overwhelming poverty and loss, WMF folks found themselves surprised by the gift of friendship in community. Not only did they encounter Jesus among people who are poor and learn to bear witness to hope in some of the world's most hopeless places, they also became recipients of the gift of friendship.

BECOMING FRIENDS: CHRISTINE'S ACCOUNT

When I first encountered folks from WMF, I was surprised—surprised by their distinctive tenderness toward children who live on the street and women who prostitute. I was surprised by how young the staff members and the organization were, and by how deeply committed they were to Jesus and to ministry with vulnerable persons. I was surprised by how they were both sober and playful, passionate and tender, idealistic and realistic. Their willingness to take risks seemed to be matched by the tenacity of their commitment and their concern for the well-being of each staff member. I was surprised by how readily they moved between Wilmore, Kentucky and the streets of Galați, Romania, or the neighborhoods of Chennai, India. I was surprised by their capacity to live in settings of enormous loss and pain, and to reflect on their experiences with faith and insight.

I was surprised by how seriously they took their relationships—the ways in which they were committed to one another and to the folks among whom they ministered. Their determined commitment to be a community and to minister in community was striking. They made organizational choices that showed how seriously they took these commitments.

About ten years ago, I met Phileena and Chris Heuertz in Wilmore. To me, they were an immediate treasure, a young and vibrant couple called to lead an extraordinary community. As we talked, and as I got to know other staff members, especially Daphne Eck Coppock, I discovered a group of folks who were doing mission and ministry a little differently. As an ethicist and a Christian, I was challenged by their willingness to dive into the ambiguities and to absorb the tensions of working in some of the hardest places. I treasured their hunger for spiritual growth and their desire for human flourishing. I was also concerned about them as individuals—wondering what the blessing and the toll of such work would look like down the road.

As I got to know Chris better, I was fascinated by his insatiable practice of reading and study coupled with the practice of ministry. He seemed to move easily between a close reading of a book by Jürgen Moltmann and responding to the very practical needs of an eight-year-old orphan in India. He and the WMF community seemed to be seeking to embody a form of life that was deep and broad—deeply rooted in the Christian tradition and turned toward community and the world's most vulnerable people.

I began to help with editing *The Cry*—WMF's quarterly journal. As I carefully read each issue, I often wept. The stories—from the field—of hurt and hope, grace and disappointment, goodness and evil touched me deeply. They were truth-filled. I was moved by staff members' commitment to living hospitably in difficult environments. Through the articles, I also began to understand the missional and spiritual identity of this organization—their lifestyle distinctives and their spiritual disciplines.

So when our mutual friend Chris Rice offered Chris and me the opportunity to write a small book together, it seemed too good to pass up. Years ago, I too had ministered in some hard places. My academic work on hospitality and other practices of community grew out of those experiences of ministry and the questions and insights they provoked. This was an opportunity to reflect on some additional experiences, especially in relation to friendship.

BECOMING FRIENDS: CHRIS'S ACCOUNT

Ten years ago, my wife, Phileena, and I spent the good part of a year living in community in Lima, Peru, with WMF staff members. Adriana and Walter Forcatto opened their home to us, a small gesture that changed us forever. During the seven months we spent in the city, countless visitors showed up at their apartment. Women and children who lived and worked on the streets would regularly stop by to see Adriana and Walter, sometimes to hang out and sometimes because they needed help to buy medicine or bus fare.

The Forcattos embodied an authentic spirituality of hospitality; their home was a safe and open place for the friends and strangers who came—literally—at any hour of the day or night.

I remember a few nights when we were awakened by cries and real emergencies. Once, a young friend came to the flat with her two-month-old baby girl. Earlier that evening, her boyfriend had beaten her viciously, splitting open a huge gash under her left eye. She needed immediate medical attention and stitches, but because she lived on the streets, she was denied admission at a local hospital. Walter and I stayed up all night with her, taking her to another hospital where we made sure she received treatment.

Experiences like that had a profound impact on me. I grew to admire and respect Adriana and Walter as I watched them love their friends.

During that time I reread Christine's book, *Making Room: Recovering Hospitality as a Christian Tradition*.[1] In it, she reflects on one of the distinctive marks of the early church: hospitality. The book takes abstract thoughts on hospitality and sets them in context. Her book was informative, but more than that, inspiring. We passed it around WMF. It fueled the souls of many in our community and challenged us to live more authentically into the grace of hospitality. Her reflections provoked our community's imagination to open our hearts even wider to the possibility of Christ visiting us in the disguise of a stranger.

We were caught off guard. A book written by an ethicist on an ancient practice of the church became a critical missional text for us. It stretched our imaginations and challenged us to evaluate donor-recipient roles in the history of mission. Practicing hospitality became a central qualifier of our community, in large part because of Christine's book.

Living with the Forcattos, I felt as if I were an eyewitness to what hospitality looked like when it was lived out. Simultaneously reading and reflecting on what Christine had written about in her book filled me with hope.

I decided to write Christine a note, introducing myself and thanking her for writing *Making Room*. I let her know how helpful it had been for our community. I hoped my e-mail to her didn't come across as "fan mail," but as an honest attempt at gratitude for her work and the gift it had become for our community. I didn't really expect to hear back from her.

But in June of 2000, she replied to my message. And I still have a copy of what she wrote. She closed with a line that I believe is what brings us together in this book. She wrote, "I pray God will continue to bless your life and ministry—especially as you continue to develop and encourage those deep friendships with the poor."

Together in this book we are trying to tease out a bit more of what that prayer means.

ON WRITING A BOOK TOGETHER

Over the years, we've been in conversation about mission, social ministry and practices that build and break community. Writing a book together is a continuation of a conversation that started a decade ago. Although our contexts are different, we have many shared understandings and commitments, and one of the delights of the project has been to recognize our own thoughts as they have been articulated or reinforced through the words and experiences of the other person.

The Resources for Reconciliation book series pairs a practitioner and an academic to reflect on an aspect of reconciliation. Certainly in how we are presently situated, those titles reflect much of our experience. But the reality is more blurred—Christine spent years as a practitioner before moving into the academy, and Chris is very much a self-taught scholar. The difference is significant, however, for the stories in this book—most are drawn from the mission experiences within WMF.

Some communities live into ministry and mission so intensely that they encounter challenges, truths and blessing more immediately and more fully than most of us whose lives are more moderate. I (Christine) have tended to learn the most from those who minister in hard places. The needs are stark, human resilience is striking, and the necessity for the work of God is so obvious. A combination of hearing about and reflecting on experiences can reshape us. They can provide a clarity of vision and a reorientation of moral imagination that allow us to look at our ordinary circumstances differently.

Once our eyes are opened to the importance of friendship, fidelity and respect in difficult situations, we can become more sensitive to them in ministry on a college campus or in a seminary environment. Mission in our neighborhoods or social ministry across town can be reframed when we recognize that friendship and love belong at the heart of every Christian ministry and act of reconciliation. Reconciliation requires friendship wherever we find ourselves. Friendships that cross the divisions of class, education, race, gender, ethnicity, age and ability are crucial for reconciliation and for the life of the church.

Stories help us understand what difference friendship makes. Because the stories in this book are primarily drawn from the life and experience of Chris and other WMF staff members, we could mistakenly conclude that we have to go far away to share in the gifts of friendship with persons who are vulnerable. But every community has people who are invisible or overlooked, and each of us can move toward wholeness through the friendships we offer and receive.

Mission or ministry with people who are poor or vulnerable often assumes that "our" task is to meet "their" needs. Whether their need is for the good news of Christ or for bread and a place to sleep, we tend to think that we have the resources and they have the needs. A focus on friendship rearranges our assumptions. *What if the resources they have also meet our needs? What if Jesus is already present in ways that will minister to us? What if in sharing life together as friends we all move closer to Jesus' heart?*

Academic conversations about mission today are sensitive to many of the issues we raise. Our work is not intended as a critique of what is being done in the academy or in mission organizations. In both social ministry and mission, however, some old paradigms are not adequate. In recent years, models of social ministry have been criticized for reinforcing social distance between providers and recipients and for offering care without respect. There are similar concerns in mission work. We hope to address some of these issues by focusing on friendship.

Many writers and practitioners, streams of thought and models of ministry have shaped each of us. Because both of us share an appreciation for John Wesley, and because he placed a distinctive emphasis on friendship with people who are poor, we have been more explicit about drawing from him than from some of the other important resources that have contributed to our thinking.

Each of us has learned from the other, and each of us has been changed by the other person's work. Our hope is that in drawing together our experiences, reflections and study, we can offer some insights into mission and ministry that are useful to the church. Though most of the stories are told in Chris's voice, the book is a fully shared project, and the stories provided the text out of which both of us worked.

When a book is written about mission and reconciliation among the poorest and most vulnerable people, and when it is devoted to exploring the significance of friendship across multiple boundaries, the very emphasis on the importance of "the poor" can reinforce conventional categories of otherness. It is easy to slip into one more version of "us and them," the very pattern we are trying to break down. Several things can help us avoid this tendency: remembering our own vulnerability, dependence and need for community, being truthful, and practicing confession and forgiveness.

Truthfulness requires that we acknowledge some differences. WMF staff members, the two of us and most of our readers have many personal assets, choices, connections and resources. These are blessings in our lives that have shaped us and our life opportunities. Even when we choose to minister among the most vulnerable communities, we never give up all of our resources. We do not experience poverty in the same way as our friends who are socioeconomically poor, and our friendships are made more complex by some of the differences. But that is only part of the story, because the ways God works in and through us are much more connected to tender hearts and open hands than to personal assets and skills. Our completeness is found in Christ and community where distinctions in status or resources mean much less.

In the chapters that follow, we will address some of these concerns from a variety of angles. We will look at the importance of relationships and community for mission, the ways that friendship helps connect personal righteousness and social justice, the gift of mutuality within friendship, the ambiguities and tensions we encounter in our efforts at reconciliation, and the spiritual resources we need for faithfulness and friendship.

I

The Vocation of Relationship

*I*n Macau, there is a cemetery filled with the graves of women and men who came to China as missionaries during the early 1900s. Most of them had lived only a few years in their new and unfamiliar environment. Their grave markers stand as a stark reminder of the history of Christian mission—a legacy often marked by great personal sacrifice.

Missionaries to Africa during that same time period faced similar hardships. With a profound awareness of the costs involved, some women and men packed their belongings in coffins, moving to Africa with the expectation of dying there. And many did, their lives and ministries on the continent shortened by disease and tragedy.

We have come a long way since then. Most people serving in mission today don't move to a foreign country expecting to be buried there. Immunizations and advances in health care reduce some of the risks. Air travel allows easier access in and out. Mission organizations work hard to ensure that crosscultural service is physically, emotionally, mentally and spiritually sustainable. Developments in technology mean missionaries don't wait months for a word from home; it is now possible to talk with family members halfway round the world as if they were across town.

But in the meantime, the mission enterprise itself has come under cultural, theological and political criticism. Mission organizations face complex questions about their roles and responsibilities in relation to local churches and leadership. Increasing sensitivity to the tendency to export a particular culture along with the gospel has challenged groups to rethink many of their mission paradigms.

Although resources have dramatically improved the sustainability of missionary service, it is increasingly rare to find people vocationally committed to the traditional "career missionary" lifetime of ministry. Today, the models are often short term—a few years in a place or perhaps a few short-term mission trips.

When we were exploring the possibility of mission as vocation, I (Chris) and my wife, Phileena, visited friends in Hong Kong. They had spent nearly forty years serving as missionaries in India, China, Taiwan and Hong Kong. As we discussed with them the possibility of serving in a missional community, they were encouraged that young people were still considering long-term mission work. Perhaps to inspire us, or perhaps to help us count the cost, they took us to the cemetery in Macau for a time of sobering reflection. They told us the story about the coffins.

As Phileena and I considered our call to mission, the notion of it becoming our "career" seemed stifling. We were the poster children of postmodern Gen Xers. From the start, we rejected the career paradigm and opted for an approach to mission that was more identified with community.

For us, a focus on career seemed to suggest that we would become specialists in evangelism or mission and that we would go to a foreign land or inner city and be the designated workers for the kingdom. We were uncomfortable with a model that made us "special" and left most Christians able to stay at home to pursue their careers confident that someone else was doing mission or looking after "those poor people" far away.

We were looking for a model that connected mission to everyday life and that located mission and ministry within community. We quickly discovered that for us this would mean moving back and forth between multiple worlds, not being specialists but dwelling with and becoming bridges between several communities.

Community would become our starting point in mission. Community would inform what we did and how we lived into our vocations of service. As we found ourselves given the opportunity to rebuild the missional organization Word Made Flesh, a central commitment to the ideals and practice of community shaped our decisions and choices.

Of course, career missionaries also had strong commitments to community. Those who lasted on the mission field usually had found ways to live in community—with the local people or in missionary compounds. Attrition was often tied to breakdowns in relationships. But we were looking for a model that was built on friendships and connections—among churches and friends in the United

States, with fellow staff members of WMF, and with the people with whom we located ourselves in other places.

From the start, our emphasis on community included rejecting certain assumptions that had shaped some mission approaches: that gifts flow in one direction only and that a substantial social distance between donors and recipients is necessary if not good. We were particularly troubled by the unintended consequences that followed from these assumptions—efforts to love "the stranger" while remaining separate from her or his life, reducing "the poor" to objects of charity, and the deep loneliness often experienced by Christians "on the mission field."

Instead, we've tried to cultivate a shared life right in the midst of the most needy and marginalized persons and communities. No compounds, but life as neighbors and friends; not trying to do it as individuals, but together building community by being community.

It wouldn't be entirely honest to suggest that we are consistently able to do community well. The wounded humanity in each of us often collides with the wounded humanity in our sisters and brothers in community. We've had to learn to fight fair. We've had to learn more about ourselves so we can understand each other better. We've made lots of mistakes, sometimes offering each other grace—other times aggravating our mistakes with new ones. But in the end, community has become an identifier of who we are and how we do mission.

Although *community* seems to have become a buzzword in contemporary Christianity, some of the most successful Christian nonprofits today are "cause-driven" organizations. Some have become wildly popular and surprisingly successful, occasionally generating more income than they can use themselves. They have become funding sources for other communities *doing* the work that the causes are generating interest around.

Cause-driven models of mission, advocacy and relief often allow contributors/donors to provide help at a distance, captured by the concern but disconnected from the actual persons most affected by it. There are so many crises and hotspots around the world that it is very easy to simply move from one cause to the next, responding to whatever is currently most pressing or compelling. Nevertheless, whether the cause is human trafficking, environmental devastation, natural disasters, genocide or famine, committed Christians recognize that focused attention and advocacy can generate widespread support.

MOVING FROM CAREER, COMMUNITY AND CAUSE TO FRIENDSHIP

Career missionaries, community-based mission and cause-driven models—each of these approaches to mission has strengths and weaknesses, especially in how they are actually lived out. Negotiating the career, community and cause continuum has taught us some important lessons.

Nearly twenty years after WMF started, we're finally realizing the significance of long-term commitment and readiness to sacrifice that stands behind the career missionary model. Today we hope that many of our staff members will see their work in WMF as a long-term calling. We grieve the loss of staff who serve with us for a number of years and then move on to other things. We often feel as if we've lost family members in their departures. We've also increasingly learned that the vulnerable women and children among whom we serve cannot afford another painful goodbye in the sad series of losses that characterize their lives.

We've discovered that our commitment to community building requires fidelity over time—fidelity to our fellow staff members and fidelity to the men, women and children who have befriended us and whom we have befriended. The work is slow, small and often undramatic. We've learned that short-term models of mission— whether in the form of week-long mission trips or one- or two-year commitments to serve—might be workable in certain situations, but in ministry with the most vulnerable people, a community has to be prepared to stay. It takes years to build the kind of relationships that result in transformation.

We are also now being challenged to help cause-driven volunteers find their way into meaningful, life-giving relationships. This has opened up new conversations related to vocational exploration and commitment. It has not been easy, and finding ways to harness the cause-driven energy of today's young people and move it toward sustained friendship in community is among our greatest challenges. We've also had to work carefully to help some WMF interns and staff members recognize that those among whom we serve are not causes or even the "human faces" of poverty, but people who have become friends.

We have found that our friends who are poor—those who suffer and are exploited—are some of our best helpers in discerning how we should enter and live within our vocations. Through these friendships, we have learned a new kind of accountability and integrity in how we think about our careers, our communities and our causes.

RELATIONSHIP WITH GOD IS AT THE HEART OF IT ALL

Behind the emphasis on friendship and community in mission stands the experience of our relationship with God. Knowing God as one who desires and offers friendship with us powerfully expands our understanding of God as Creator, Judge, Redeemer and Lover of our souls.

We don't usually think of God as having friends, but several times Abraham is described as being God's friend (2 Chronicles 20:7; Isaiah 41:8; James 2:23). Abraham—mostly faithful, generous and obedient but also imperfect and prone to taking short-cuts— is described as one chosen to "keep the way of the Lord by doing righteousness and justice" (Genesis 18:19). Abraham's life was transformed by his relationship with God. He followed God to a new place and a new role; he was chosen and willing to be part of God's purposes. And God was remarkably faithful to Abraham, confiding in him, rescuing him and blessing him.

Jesus calls his disciples friends rather than servants because of shared commitments and purposes (John 15:7-17). The love that Jesus commands his friends to have is the love that he is about to show them. "No one has greater love than this," he explains, "to lay down one's life for one's friends." The linking of sacrificial love and friendship is key for his disciples, and the result is joy, lasting fruit and a love that endures.

When Jesus is called a friend of tax collectors and sinners, the description is not intended as a compliment (Matthew 11:19; Luke 7:34). But it does acknowledge the shocking welcome he embodied in reaching out to those considered unclean and unworthy. He seems to have enjoyed being with them. Causing considerable offense to the religious authorities, Jesus gladly shared meals with these friends and brought them love, hope and healing. And they often embraced him with dramatic generosity and powerful spiritual insight.

Friends of God love what and whom God loves. The Scriptures make clear that God's love is abundant and available for each of us, but also that in a particular and protective way God loves those who are most vulnerable: widows, orphaned children, strangers and those pushed to the margins of a community.[1]

Jesus offers us friendship, and that gift shapes a surprisingly subversive missional paradigm. A grateful response to God's gift of friendship involves offering that same gift to others—whether family or strangers, coworkers or children who live on the street. Offering and receiving friendship breaks down the barriers of "us" and "them" and opens up possibilities of healing and reconciliation.

CONTEMPORARY COLLISIONS

Learning to see the so-called other as a friend increases our sensitivity to the reductionism, commodification and manipulation that plague some versions of mission and ministry. Human beings who are not Christians are far more than potential converts. In our concern for reaching out with the gospel, we can unwittingly reduce the person to less than the whole being that God formed. When we shrink our interest in people to the possibilities of where their souls may spend eternity, it is easy to miss how God might already be working in and through a particular person. We are better able to resist tendencies to reductionism when we are in relationships that affirm each person's dignity and identity and when we come into those relationships confident that God is already at work in the other person.

Because a business mindset is so prevalent in our society, the work of mission is sometimes recast in very economic terms. Missional language like "target audience" and a focus on results-driven measurements echo a sales approach that sees people first as potential consumers—in this case, consumers of the product we're offering, a particular version of Christianity.

Such approaches open us to the temptation toward manipulation, and manipulation should never be mistaken for evangelism. Unfortunately, certain types of strategic outreach assume that the means don't matter if the end result is good. But the means and ends are profoundly intertwined. If we want people to experience the kingdom of God and to dwell with God for eternity, then how they experience their relationship with us should be a foretaste of that goodness and beauty.

The very content of the good news helps us resist temptations to overlook the connection between the goal and means of mission. To understand mission and evangelism, we need to recover a fuller understanding of the good news itself: the gift of God to humanity expressed in the incarnation of Christ.

It is surprisingly easy to lose sight of the close connection between the good news and evangelism or mission. But the term "evangelizing" comes from the Greek verb *euangelizo,* which is translated as announcing the "gospel" or the "good news." In his book *Announcing the Reign of God: Evangelization and the Subversive Memory of Jesus,* Bishop Mortimer Arias notes that prior to the incarnation of Christ, *euangelizo*[2] had primarily been used in a political context. Before Jesus announced that the kingdom of God had come, *euangelizo* typically referred to the overthrow of an established government, the proclamation of a victory in battle or the return of the emperor. The concept conjured up images of a regime change.[3]

Significant implications follow for how we understand our call to live out the good news. The kingdom of God came into conflict with the empire—the kingdom of humanity. It follows that we would see evangelism and mission as life on the frontlines of kingdom-level conflict and missionaries and evangelists as subversives. But subversion is not usually our first image when we think of mission or evangelism.

What is it that we are subverting, and what kind of subversion are we called to, especially in relation to the mission of reconciliation? Part of the subversion involves restoring relationships to the center of our lives, ministry and mission. Friendships that open into reconciliation validate the message of the good news. Our practice becomes inseparable from our message, and affirming the divine imprint of God in each human being compels us to love as an extension of God's love at work in us.

Locating friendship at the heart of mission involves certain assumptions—that reconciliation with God is something for which every human being is made and that relationships are reciprocal. Mission, then, is less about our efforts to help or evangelize "them," and more about how we can live into the kingdom together. Friendship puts the focus on relationships and offers an alternative to models of mission that are more formal, professional or bureaucratic. In the career model, missionaries have sometimes found themselves working as professional program administrators, quite distant from the people to whom they were called. The greater the distance and the more complex the work, the harder it can be to assume that local relationships matter, that they might be interesting or satisfying, or that they are important to one's own relationship to God. Such distancing also makes it harder to resist turning people into projects and drives us to find our support and identity in our friendships with other missionaries or coworkers.

The possibility of and longing for local friendships is what drew many present staff members to WMF. Much like career missionaries, we learned to love those we had gone to serve. But as the friendships on the streets and in the neighborhoods grew, we came to understand that we were not ministering "to" our friends, but in ministry "among" them. We ourselves were being ministered *to* as authentic and humanizing relationships emerged.

REDEFINING SUCCESS

As our friendships grew and deepened, we discovered that we loved the people among whom we lived and ministered. We looked forward to having dinner with Mansoor and his family; we drew joy from being included in Sujana's celebrations. We were transformed by sharing life with Gautam and Rekha Rai and their children. Gradually we realized that even more than we wanted to "minister" to our friends, we wanted to be in community with them.

This shift in orientation brought us into conflict with certain mission paradigms that approached these contexts with a need/ solution mentality. Our experience of reciprocal benefit and blessing involved solidarity and mutual transformation. By embracing incarnation, simplicity and gritty grassroots experience, we were finding and sharing life.

It was hard to think of our friends primarily as potential converts or as a target audience. We became uncertain about what it might mean to keep statistics on our successes. Our love for Christ and our experience of Christ's love for us motivated and compelled us to make the crosscultural moves that we did. Enthralled by Jesus' goodness and beauty, we wanted everyone to know him. But we didn't want to compromise the integrity of Jesus' goodness or our friendships by using them strategically. We wanted to live into the beauty of Christ's love by being faithful to how we understood it had been offered to us.

We were surprised. In relationships and friendships with those who are poor, we were learning to follow our friends to God's heart. Along the way, we redefined success in terms of faithfulness.

That's what we learned from the model of Christ. Jesus chose twelve disciples and called them friends, but on the night he was arrested, his friends failed him miserably: Judas betrayed him, Peter denied him three times, and the others abandoned him. Even after Jesus' resurrection, Thomas doubted him. If an assessment were done shortly after the crucifixion, the numbers weren't there for success. Ultimately, eleven of the twelve "finished strong," but how do we measure success in the midst of ministry?

Was Jesus "successful" in his calling, mentoring, training and sending of the twelve disciples? When do we take the measurements? What do we measure? Perhaps "success" is the wrong category. Jesus was *faithful*. Even to the end of Judas's life, Jesus loved him.

Success doesn't make sense of a self-giving love that is offered even to those who betray, deny, abandon and doubt us. But according to Scripture, faithfulness in loving our friends—whether or not we see immediate results—does yield a harvest of fruit. And together we are drawn closer to the heart of God.

Confronting Our Idealism

A model of mission focused on relationship, friendship and reconciliation generated a lot of positive momentum at the start. To embody an alternative to convert-driven success models seemed subversive and exciting. But the actual reality of forming friendships was more complicated.

Back in 1994, I (Chris) helped start what we understand to be the first pediatric AIDS care home in South Asia. We cared for girls and boys who were HIV positive and those who had been orphaned because their parents had died from AIDS. In staffing the home, we created a restorative component for young women and girls who had escaped the commercial sex industry. Many of them, considered fugitives by their former pimps and brothel owners, needed a safe haven far from their previous homes. We offered them the chance to reclaim their lives and identities. There were jobs to do and counseling opportunities available. The community provided space and support as our new friends tried to recover from years of sexual abuse and physical trauma.

But each woman had been deeply wounded by her experiences. Many struggled with trust and fearfully held on to what little they had. Others were still angry.

We were astonished when Maya, one of our friends, betrayed us. She had a job, a safe place, a warm bed and the possibility of starting over. She was the first, but other women followed, robbing the children's home and fleeing with clothing, kitchen utensils or the petty cash from the office. We would wake in the morning to find an empty bed and plundered shelves. Another new friend had disappeared into the night. We rarely saw them again.

Recognizing the detrimental effects this kind of behavior could have on the children, we discussed whether or not it was wise to welcome into the home women who were escaping from the commercial sex industry. We ourselves started experiencing a form of attachment disorder—how many times could we handle being betrayed and abandoned by people we were befriending?

Our idealism in offering friendship started wearing thin, but our experience of Christ's love and his love for each person compelled us to keep at it. We also gradually realized that we would need to come to terms with our own brokenness, with the ways we betrayed, doubted and denied God's love for us and the love of our brothers and sisters.

Slowly we were being reconciled to God's vision of faithfulness and love. Through the pain of loss we came to realize the joy of giving ourselves in love and friendship. The pain was an indicator that the friendship had become meaningful to us.

Of course, there were plenty of other instances when women stayed with us, cared faithfully for the children, and found hope and healing in the community. Many from Hindu and Muslim backgrounds came to faith in Christ and were baptized.

Another challenge to faithfulness and friendship emerged at this point. Some folks wanted us to tell the success stories and publish the pictures of the women's baptisms. We resisted.

In these new relationships we were still exploring the limits of trust and the meaning of friendship. It seemed to us that posting pictures of the women in a newsletter or on a website risked commodifying their stories and exploiting their pain.[4] They were not the "converted fruits" of our labor; they were friends we love, whatever their response to us.

Surprised by How Long Things Take

Nearly fifteen years later, many of our friends who had experienced trauma and abuse are still struggling to find wholeness. Long-term friendships have shown that there isn't a quick fix or an easy answer to their pain. While some have experienced miraculous emotional healing, others have prayed and prayed, but still can't seem to get past some of the wounds that scar their souls. Recovery may well take a lifetime.

The career mentality that had initially seemed stifling to us has now become an invitation to fidelity in friendship. Can we remain faithful to our friends who have trusted us with the most vulnerable parts of their lives? Will our own community be able to resist turning them into the "flesh and blood" stories for a cause that will bring attention and advocacy on their behalf? We've been surprised by how strong the internal and external pressure is to use vulnerable people for "good" purposes.

Our friendships are inviting us into a faithfulness that looks a lot like a calling or vocation—determined for us by the very relationships we have formed.

The emphasis on friendship, simplicity, living "in the neighborhood" alongside children who live on the street, and the gritty reality of finding beauty and building community in the hard places has resonated with the imagination of some young people interested in mission. We've been surprised by the number of internship and staff applications that have come from the grown children of presidents of some major evangelical missions agencies. Drawn to a lifestyle that embodies a different approach to mission, they challenge us to define how we are different from traditional models of mission. Simultaneously they remind us how much we stand on the shoulders of their parents and grandparents.

Just as we are looking for people who are willing to make long-term commitments to community, the most recent applicants to WMF bring their focus on causes. To move forward, we'll need to draw strengths from the career, community and cause emphases, being careful to keep our focus on friendship. Our friends are not projects or personal embodiments of a cause, but partners in community.

INDICATORS OF THE INTEGRITY OF OUR FRIENDSHIPS

How can we tell if we've turned individual people into projects or representatives of causes? Are there indicators of friendships at the margins? Do certain practices reveal understandings of evangelism and mission that are at odds with friendship?

One simple test of integrity is what we write in our prayer and support letters. Can we imagine the letters being read by the people among whom we serve?

Sometimes the letters are shockingly transparent—about *other* people's lives. In an effort to raise financial support or encourage prayer, the vulnerabilities of other people's lives are exposed—stories of addiction, abuse, sexual indiscretion, crisis and all sorts of personal information are revealed. Once written, but then mailed or e-mailed to hundreds of people, the intimate details of the letters are usually framed as prayer requests. But often the details are shared without permission, and the person whose story is being told knows little about how his or her struggle and transformation have been recounted.

Prayer letters are second only to PowerPoint presentations in their potential for violating friendship. Imagine how you would feel if your worst moment (a day when bad hair, no sleep and difficult circumstances combined to make you look terrible) was photographed and then displayed during Sunday morning worship.

During short-term mission trips, it is particularly tempting to engage in some version of travel voyeurism. With little time to build relationships, well-meaning volunteers try to capture their experience by taking pictures of cute kids or deplorable slums. The more desperate the scene, the more persuasive the message when they return home. As photos are processed or e-mailed back home and passed around churches and supporters, the implicit message is to see the suffering of the "other" or peek into their unguarded lives and respond by saying, "We really do take a lot for granted."

There's no doubt that pictures of friends and family are a treasure—when we take them and use them for the right reasons. We take photos because we want to preserve the memories of special times together with people we love. We eagerly share the photos with them to celebrate our appreciation for their presence in our lives. Similarly we are happy to share information about friends and family with other people we love, but it is important to do it with care and respect. Just as we are put off by family Christmas letters that overstate how well everyone is doing, mission prayer letters can be untruthful in how they overstate successes or desperate circumstances.

Years ago when I (Christine) worked for Bread for the World, a Christian citizens' advocacy group on hunger issues, I learned to be very careful about how concern was raised about people who were hungry. BFW explicitly avoided publishing distressing pictures of individuals in need, unwilling to contribute to what has sometimes been called "hunger pornography." It is tempting to capture a portion of human experience at the expense of the whole to accomplish some other purpose. Hunger, exploitation or need may be part of someone's experience, but it does not define them.

It can be very helpful to imagine that those about whom you are speaking or for whom you are advocating are in your presence. To imagine them present provides a discipline on how we speak of others and the problems they face. I (Christine) have been challenged a number of times, when teaching on offering hospitality to vulnerable guests, to have some of those "guests" in my audience. It changes how you think and say things about people who are homeless or people with disabilities when they are present, listening to and engaging your words. If they cannot be present, imagining them as participants in the conversation provides a holy discipline that only friendship can fully provide.

A commitment to friendship also challenges particular evangelism strategies, especially those that involve very brief encounters with strangers. Short forays downtown with a handful of tracts to do street witnessing can reflect very reductionist understandings of the gospel as well as a reductionist view of human beings. Armed with opening lines to start the conversation, eager young evangelists sometimes probe into the most intimate places of potential converts' lives, asking them about their morality, fears and sins and offering a chance of forgiveness. In the brief encounter, people are invited to confess their sins to complete strangers and give the rest of their lives to a God to whom they may have been introduced only a few minutes earlier.

Even if we haven't engaged in street evangelism ourselves, most of us have been victims of overzealous street witnessing. While there are always exceptions, many of the encounters are annoying and leave us feeling a little bit violated. Part of the problem is that these encounters are rarely accompanied by any evidence of a desire for a relationship with the person who has been targeted.

It's hard to imagine why we would think that people would want a relationship with Jesus if they sensed no interest on our part in a relationship with them.

Out of her experience of ministering for decades in Hong Kong with people who were addicted to drugs, Jackie Pullinger has said, "Don't tell someone about Christ unless you're willing to give them your bed."[5] In many parts of the world a conversion to Christianity would mean isolation from one's community and even family. Jackie was on to something, in terms of the seriousness with which we might engage evangelism and the importance of new relationships. If we're really inviting someone into the family of God, then they become our family as well.

"Friendship evangelism" is another evangelistic approach very vulnerable to misuse and misinterpretation. Befriending someone *merely so you can tell them the gospel* is a form of manipulation and a violation of trust. Augustine argued that loving the neighbor meant wanting what was best for them, which is to know and to love God.[6] So desiring this for a friend is a very good thing. But it must involve more than words and strategy; it involves fidelity within the friendship itself. Real friendship leads to an ongoing community of love. Such love is self-giving and vulnerable; it puts the other person first.

Some of our approaches to conversion have earned the mistrust of the very people we want to reach. Warning signs help us see that when we depend on manipulation instead of love and on strategy instead of grace, our efforts to proclaim the good news are malformed and hurtful.

BUILDING AND SUSTAINING TRUST

Back in 1994, I (Chris) was sitting on the roof of the building where I used to live in India. I had spent a long day working at a children's home and came back to my flat just in time for the sunset. I was reading through my mail when one of my neighbors, Fakrudin, a Muslim student, came up on the terrace and introduced himself.

We spent the rest of the evening talking about movies, family and why I was living in India. The next day Fakrudin introduced me to some of his friends in the neighborhood, the Mustafa Syeds. They are a Muslim family with three sons—Mansoor, Jeelan and Adil. Their young mother, Ammi, was taking care of them alone because years before we met, their father had abandoned the family, leaving them in a slum-clearance building, the housing provided by the government after it "clears" a slum. These four young men quickly became dear friends, and over the years we have made countless memories together.

We've also made a point to keep in touch. They thoughtfully send greetings at each major milestone in my life—birthdays and anniversaries—as well as remembering to send cards, make calls or even mail gifts for all the major Christian holidays. They've scheduled their weddings around my visits to Asia so I could attend and participate. My friendship with this family has been one of the most life giving I've ever experienced.

Phileena and I regularly review our monthly missionary support statements to track our income trends, generate a list of people we want to thank and pray for, and note any variances in giving patterns. This past fall we were shocked to see that one of the names on that income report was our old neighbor Mansoor, Ammi's oldest son.

An Indian. A Muslim. A former victim of human trafficking himself. A poor person. To us, a neighbor, a friend and a brother. It was Mansoor.

Is Mansoor the "target audience"—part of a mission emphasis on reaching Muslims? Is his story of bonded labor and human slavery (see chap. 4) one that needs to be told as part of generating awareness of a cause with which we need to be aligned? Is he a donor, a supporter of our work? Most fundamentally, Mansoor is my friend, part of my community.

Mansoor and I have some fundamental disagreements when it comes to society, politics, economics and, of course, religion. But we've committed to an ongoing process of reconciling the differences between us. We've spent fifteen years building trust and sustaining that trust. We talked about sharing his story and he was glad to give permission. I have no suspicions that Mansoor is secretly or discreetly trying to convert me to Islam, though I'm sure he'd be delighted with the possibility of sharing our faith traditions. And though I'd love for Mansoor to know the love of God through the person of Jesus, I'm committed to him whether or not he accepts Christianity. I know he trusts my friendship with him, one that is motivated by God's love for all of us—one that affirms God's imprint on all humanity.

Being in community with Mansoor, and sharing our broader communities with each other, is part of doing life together. Our friendship has been mutually transforming—we're each different because of it. I pray God's best for him in all things, and that he would find in Christ a friendship that is unlike anything he has experienced. And yet I also trust that our friendship has given him glimpses and signs of hope that this is possible.

2

Reconnecting Righteousness and Justice Through Friendships

A few years ago, a series of commercials for a shampoo product saturated television programming. Each ad portrayed a woman experiencing sexual ecstasy as she washed her hair in the shower. Quite the product—or, at least, quite a promise.

The disconnect between our ordinary experience of hair washing and the implicit claims of the commercial is partly what made some of us laugh at the ad. When we remember that particular advertisement, or the dozens of others that are like it, we laugh or sometimes smirk. Perhaps we are also mildly shocked by the crassness, the explicit sexuality, but we don't often name the misunderstanding of sex it represents or the flippancy of our own responses. If we think about it at all, the ad is utterly ridiculous, but it is not harmless.

Around the same time that those commercials were running, a board member of Word Made Flesh traveled to Sri Lanka. She collaborated with a friend there in assisting the government as they shut down thirty children's homes. Most of them were homes for young boys.

Ordinarily the closing of children's homes would be very bad news for the vulnerable and orphaned children of Sri Lanka. Community-based, residential-care homes meet basic needs for many of them. In this case, however, it was good news—it meant freedom. The homes that were shut down were fronts for the commercial sex tourism industry. Impoverished and vulnerable little boys were essentially being kidnapped and then forced to serve as sex-slaves—primarily for European men on vacation.

Sex tourism is big business. Men from numerous so-called developed nations book their holiday package, catch a flight to Sri Lanka or another accommodating destination and check in at their resort. They then visit one of the boys' homes to select the child (or children) they prefer and take them back to their rooms. They then rape the boys, often repeatedly, throughout the duration of their vacation.

The misuse of money, sex and power is inscribed on those little bodies, over and over again. To be sure, there are local people who are complicit in this business, but that only makes the story more appalling. And the story is replicated in many other places, often with young girls—kidnapped, sold and exploited repeatedly.

When we hear about these stories or see the news reports, we are shocked, troubled, horrified. We wonder what we might do to help end modern slavery and the sexual exploitation of children. Is there a way we can help in bringing an end to such outrageous expressions of evil and injustice?

Well, we could start with not buying products that make sexuality and sexual experience a joke. Would that help? Whom would that help? It wouldn't do much for the little boys in Sri Lanka or the young girls in Thailand—at least not immediately. But perhaps by paying closer attention to advertising and entertainment, and to how morally callous we've become, we'd see things a little differently. And perhaps it would help us connect concerns about righteousness and justice a little more closely.

In our hunger to be liberated and to throw off some of the stereotypes of uptight, narrow Christians, many of us have forgotten how to blush. Advertising and much of the current entertainment world continually invite us to trivialize or misuse the God-given gift of our sexuality. The media are not alone in contributing to our moral callousness. Practices in business and politics have reinforced a shockingly greedy and self-centered approach to money and power.

Followers of Jesus could be far more attentive to the bridges between our personal lifestyle choices and the injustices around us, between our individual righteousness and our work for justice. A wholesale loss of the capacity to blush, personally and in the society at large, contributes to an environment in which the ripple effects are devastating for the most powerless among us.

Being friends with Jesus and with those who are poor requires that we give up being friends with "the world." When James writes that "friendship with the world is enmity with God" (4:4) he is warning followers of Jesus to be wary of the world's values and practices. He challenges us against adopting lifestyles of coveting, violence, self-indulgence, ambition, impurity and arrogance.

Sure, it is just a shampoo commercial, and it has little if any bearing on sexual exploitation in Sri Lanka. But when those boys or girls are our friends, and they bear the scars of sexual misuse, it makes us take a second look at how our imaginations have been shaped by careless views of sex and power.

Those men who booked vacations didn't just wake up one morning and decide that misusing the bodies of children was an acceptable form of entertainment. What in their formation and environment, in their prior choices and social experience, led them down such destructive paths? Moral callousing comes in many forms and in varying levels of intensity and destructiveness, but each of us, even as Christians, is vulnerable to blind spots regarding money, sex and power.

RIGHTEOUSNESS AND JUSTICE:
TWO SIDES OF THE SAME COIN

Today we mostly associate justice with efforts to promote equality and guarantee human rights. We connect it with advocacy for the most vulnerable and their gaining a voice, becoming full participants in a community. Justice is linked to economic, social and political power. In the United States, it is especially associated with fairness and an equitable distribution of benefits and burdens in society. Work for justice involves our efforts to right the wrongs of institutionalized inequality and oppression.

We know that the Bible calls us to stand with those who are oppressed, marginalized and powerless.[1] This involves the work of justice and reflects God's concern for the most vulnerable of the world. God assures us that the creator and sustainer of the universe will be the protector and advocate for those who have no other helper. To work for justice is to partner with God in bringing healing to the world.

Often when we think of righteousness, we associate it with an individual's behavior and his or her avoidance of worldly temptations. We locate it in particular behaviors or attitudes. Today we are more likely to hear a person described as self-righteous than as righteous. Being a righteous man or woman does not capture current understandings of goodness. We're unlikely to assume that a person's righteousness and her or his work for justice are connected.

But if we think of biblical images of a righteous person, as in the book of Job, we see that they are connected in part to personal choices about money, sex and power, the very heart of justice concerns. Job eloquently describes the practices of a righteous person—one who helps orphaned children and people who are poor, makes the "widow's heart . . . sing for joy" and champions the "cause of the stranger" (Job 29:13, 16). A righteous person is sexually chaste and faithful, just and generous toward those with little power, and trusts in God rather than wealth (Job 31).

There are certainly other aspects of these terms, such as in retributive justice that is about punishment, and imputed righteousness that is tied to Christ's work for us. But for our reflections on justice, reconciliation and friendship, the close connection between righteousness and distributive justice in Scripture is particularly important.

In Hebrew the words that are translated as righteousness and justice (*sedeqah, mispat*) and their derivatives are often used together or interchangeably. Both have to do with living justly and according to God's purposes, a rightness in relationships, a wholeness to life for the individual and the community.[2]

In his discussion of three related aspects of liberation, the Latin American theologian Gustavo Gutiérrez helps us see that our work for justice, our friendships and our personal righteousness are interrelated parts of God's work of salvation or healing. He describes (1) liberation from structural evil and exploitation—changing the political and economic structures that keep some people from life and freedom, (2) living into and participating in the inner freedom that can exist in spite of servitude—the freedom that comes with sharing life in community, building friendships, experiencing respect and telling stories of a different kind of world that is possible, and (3) liberation from personal sin that comes with salvation and sanctification in Christ.[3]

In James 1:27, religion that is pure and undefiled before God is described as caring "for orphans and widows in their distress" and keeping "oneself unstained by the world." The verse links the internal and external, attention to individual hearts and attitudes and one's posture and activity in the world. Similarly, a closer look at connections between holiness and justice in the work of God and in expectations for God's people would challenge our tendency to bifurcate personal and social concerns.

So what does this have to do with shampoo commercials and exploited children? It suggests that there might be bridges between our unrighteousness and major injustices in the world—bridges we haven't noticed or haven't chosen to notice.

Years ago the movie *Traffic* illustrated this point very concretely. The film portrayed a group of high school kids partying on the weekends, abusing cocaine and other substances to take the edge off their internal pain. Simultaneously the film documented how drug trafficking creates orphans and widows in places like Mexico City. If we were regularly reminded of the impact of our consumption patterns on the most vulnerable, would we change our practices?

In a globalized economy, it is often hard to see the connections. It takes courage and honesty to look for them and to respond with changed behavior when the people who are most affected are far away or hidden from view. We rarely think about how our minor lifestyle choices in the things we buy, the movies we choose, the language we use and the activities we find enjoyable have anything to do with other people's pain and suffering. Sometimes there is a very direct line of connection, as in drug use; sometimes it is much less explicit, as in the slow callousing that comes from the trivializing of sexual intimacy.

But even the distant connections can become very explicit and personal. It's more likely to happen when our friendships create personal pathways between wealth and poverty, and between vulnerability and power.

ENCOUNTERING THE GAP

On a recent trip to South India, I (Chris) had lunch with some old friends. We first met fifteen years ago when I was living in an apartment on the edge of the slum where they live. Devi, the youngest of five sisters, and I sat on the curb and played jacks in the street. Often in the evenings her family invited me to share a cup of tea with them or to join them in their meal. We sat and ate together on the dirt floor in their little thatched home. In many ways, they have become family to me.

They are a traditional, folk Hindu family from a rural village now living in one of India's largest cities. The three oldest daughters never had the opportunity to study beyond middle school. Their father died recently, but even when they were young, circumstances forced the girls to work in order to help provide for the rest of their family. The best jobs they could find were as seamstresses at a garment factory that supplies popular brand name clothing for companies in the United States.

While visiting them not long ago, I was wearing a red, button-down shirt I had recently bought at the Gap store in a local shopping mall in Omaha. I was hardly seated when the oldest daughter, Sujana, told me she had stitched that same shirt. She asked if she could look at the label. Sure enough, it read, "Made in India." She recognized the Gap tag immediately. She was very proud of her work. Sujana then asked how much it cost in the United States. My heart sank; I felt ashamed and uncomfortable. I knew that the forty dollars I had paid for that shirt was more than she earns in an entire month.

Sujana and her family are among our more than one billion global neighbors who barely survive on less than $1 a day. Even when I'm with them, I find it hard to comprehend their precarious economic situation. They are so hospitable, gracious and strong while they are also desperately poor.[4]

IS THE "PLUNDER FROM THE POOR" IN MY HOUSE?

Sujana and the red shirt make the judgment in Isaiah 3:14-15 very personal. The passage reads, "The plunder from the poor is in your houses. What do you mean by crushing my people and grinding the faces of the poor? declares the Lord, the Lord Almighty."[5] While God's judgment in Isaiah 2 and 3 on the arrogance of the house of Jacob is more comprehensive than this single phrase, having any role in plundering the poor is a terrifying image.

It's not often the case that we are personally confronted with the connection between our personal choices and someone else's need, but when it happens, it can be life changing. For John Wesley, it came in the form of a young woman at his door asking for help for herself and her baby. They were hungry and cold. Wesley was sympathetic but unable to give much assistance because he'd just spent almost all his available money to decorate his house. The pictures that he'd bought earlier in the day hung on his walls as lovely but painful reminders of the choices he'd made.[6]

This experience when Wesley was a young university student (and others like it) led the eighteenth-century reformer to take a very strong stand on possessions and the use of money. Because he was friends with many poor people, he found it impossible to avoid seeing their needs and his own capacity to help. Because he wanted to follow Jesus and to be like him, he shared what he had and worked tirelessly to persuade others to do the same.

Once when he was in the grip of an illness he thought would be fatal, he ordered the inscription on his tombstone to read: "Here lieth the body of John Wesley, a brand plucked out of the burning: who died of a consumption in the fifty first year of his age, not leaving, after his debts are paid, ten pounds behind him: praying, God be merciful to me, an unprofitable servant!"[7] He lived many years longer but never wavered from a commitment to keep only what he needed of his income and to give the rest away.[8]

Many of us live at a sufficient distance from people in need that our choices about how we spend our money don't hit home the way they did with Wesley and his pictures or Chris and his red shirt. But if the ancient Christian tradition is correct, that everything we have beyond necessity is not ours but given to us by God so that we can pass it on to those in need, then each of these interactions is a gift rather than a burden. They reveal to us the truth about what God intends for our resources and our lives. The ancient tradition, and later church leaders like Wesley, did not mince words; they argued that self-indulgent, uncaring use of resources steals life from poor people.[9]

Wesley could not have been more direct in the connections he made than when he wrote that every penny we spend on expensive clothing is,

> in effect, stolen from God and the poor! And how many precious opportunities of doing good have you defrauded yourself

of! How often have you disabled yourself from doing good by purchasing what you did not [need]. . . . I pray consider this well. Perhaps you have not seen it in this light before. When you are laying out that money in costly apparel which you could have otherwise spared for the poor, you thereby deprive them of what God, the proprietor of all, had lodged in your hands for their use. If so, what you put upon yourself, you are, in effect, tearing from the back of the naked; as the costly and delicate food which you eat, you are snatching from the mouth of the hungry. For mercy, for pity, for Christ's sake, for the honour of his gospel, stay your hand! Do not throw this money away! Do not lay out on nothing, yea, worse than nothing, what may clothe your poor, naked, shivering fellow-creature![10]

Does that mean that we must all sew our own clothes, or live without the beauty of artwork in our homes? Probably not, but it does suggest that if we know people who lack sufficient food, clothing or housing to sustain life, it would be harder to spend our money frivolously or self-indulgently.

The issues are complex, and Wesley described the combination of social heartlessness, spiritual apathy and greed he saw in his own day as "complicated wickedness" or "complicated villainy."[11] He regularly connected personal lifestyle decisions with spiritual health and with responding to the needs of people who were impoverished. Recognizing that indulgence and waste harmed everyone involved, he reminded his parishioners that when they used resources badly,

You bind your own hands. You make it impossible for you to do that good which otherwise you might, so that you injure the poor in the same proportion as you poison your own soul. You might have clothed the naked; but what was due to them was thrown away on your own costly apparel. You might have fed the hungry . . . but the superfluities of your own table swallowed up that whereby they should have been profited. And so this wasting of thy Lord's goods is an instance of complicated wickedness; since hereby thy poor brother perisheth, for whom Christ died.[12]

In response to the excuse offered by those with resources that they don't know anyone in need of help, Wesley explained, "One great reason why the rich, in general, have so little sympathy for the poor is because they so seldom visit them. Hence it is that . . . one part of the world does not know what the other suffers. Many of them do not know, because they do not care to know: they keep out of the way of knowing it; and then plead their voluntary ignorance as an excuse for their hardness of heart."[13]

Voluntary ignorance is as dangerous as it is easy. Choosing not to see and avoiding thinking about the consequences of our decisions or lifestyles do not make us blameless. Opening our eyes to the global realities and moving beyond our areas of comfort can become avenues leading to deeper discipleship, compassion and justice.

Sujana and her sisters work for pennies an hour to clothe folks who can spend between $40 and $120 on a shirt or pair of pants. The global economics are complicated, but it is not hard to see that the overall system is still dependent on plundering the poorest.

What can be done? Can a friendship with Sujana and her sisters change our perspective or practice? Can her story draw us closer to God and to God's priorities?

BRIDGING THE GAP

In a small and personal attempt to bridge the disparity between Sujana's family and my own, I (Chris) bought some stock in Gap Inc. (GPS) hoping that it would go up. My plan was to sell that stock and give the profits to Sujana and her family—a sort of "profit sharing" idea. Ironically, the stock's value has been sliding downward ever since.[14]

On a recent trip to India, I asked the girls again about their jobs and how things have been for them. They were glad to talk about their circumstances. Sujana and her sister Bhindu (who has subsequently stopped working) have worked at the same garment factory for over ten years and are making 3,000 Indian rupees a month (roughly $69.00, or $0.26 an hour). A younger sister, Nadikah, who has been working there for four years, is making 2,500 rupees (about $57.00 a month or $0.22 an hour).

They are grateful for their salaries since a first-year employee makes only 1,400 rupees a month ($32.00 or $0.12 an hour). Even that is far more than their mother makes as she sits on the side of a busy road and sells strands of jasmine flowers that women wear in their hair; she gets about $0.11 for every yard of flowers she braids and sells. But even the wages paid by the garment factory aren't enough to provide for a family of six. In fact, with their incomes combined, the family survives on about $0.70 per person per day—

in a country where gasoline costs $5.00 (U.S.) a gallon.

Sujana recently bought a skirt she had sewn at work. The factory sometimes lets employees buy pieces with minor defects at discounted rates. This particular skirt had two red stains, but Sujana was delighted that two of her younger sisters could share it. While admiring Sujana's work, I noticed the label inside the skirt. It read "Eddie Bauer." I told her that I knew of that clothing company and asked what other companies Sujana's factory supplied. In her broken English and my limited Tamil, I figured out that she has recently made clothes for Eddie Bauer, J. Jill, Old Navy, Gap and Banana Republic. In fact, she was proud to find out that Banana Republic was a legitimate brand (I think the name might have thrown her).

Sujana then explained that she and her sister work ten hours a day, six days a week. They receive no health care benefits, and there is no pension plan for employees. Although they are given days off for a few public and religious holidays, they have no vacation.

Friendship with Sujana and her family make the ethical issues associated with multinational corporations very personal. The power and resources of these corporations, for good and ill, to shape the lives of workers who produce goods for them is extraordinary. In some cases, the assets of a single multinational corporation exceed those of a national government.

When corporations and the local companies associated with them take advantage of the needs and vulnerabilities of people who are desperate for a way out of the harshest poverty, they too plunder the poor. As consumers, we benefit from this hidden exploitation.

We're unlikely to give up our benefits or challenge corporations to pay just wages unless we come face-to-face with the human toll.

FACING OUR TANGLED CONSUMPTION PATTERNS

Even after all these years of friendship with Sujana, at some point, I (Chris) will probably shop again at the Gap, Old Navy or Banana Republic (I have a few Gap gift cards in my wallet). After the stories and critique, I know it seems like a sellout. But to be honest, my practices are conflicted and not always consistent.

Whether it's the Gap or Macy's, Target or Home Depot, in a globalized economy, we need to be asking questions about how products have been made, the conditions for the workers and the impact on the environment. Almost all of us can become more careful about what we purchase and how we use our resources. We can eat "lower on the food chain" or, in Wesley's terms, "less delicately," we can make better use of secondhand stores, and be more creative about housing options and sharing appliances. We can surely work harder to resist the cultural messages that continually proclaim that more is better and new is best.

While we may not be able to break free entirely from buying products made under unjust circumstances, we can make many decisions that will matter. And to conclude that withdrawing from the economy entirely or giving in to consumerism are our only options may be the most problematic posture of all.

Much work remains to be done at the national and international levels with corporations, governments and advocacy organizations. Efforts to change public and corporate policies require our steady, patient work and determined, intelligent and organized action. Decisions by multinational companies and by individual governments affect the most vulnerable, and small changes at the macro level can have important effects around the world.

Organized efforts can be effective, though the issues are sufficiently complex that finding real solutions, beyond registering protest, is difficult and requires solid understandings of global economics and their human impact. If we boycotted all the companies that have their clothing lines made in India, the companies that manufacture their clothes in Thailand and Cambodia would remain. Sometimes singling out certain companies or industries for criticism seems to open us up to new forms of inconsistency.

In other cases, it is not necessarily easy to identify the "good guys." Some of the most popular "made in America" brands on the market today tout the fact that they don't use sweatshop labor, but then they go on to push the boundaries of child pornography in their advertising campaigns. Exploiting sweatshop labor or exploiting sexuality in advertising seem like two bad choices for consumers.

Nevertheless, there are advocacy groups that do trustworthy research and responsible policy development and they can offer guidance.[15] We can't all become experts in global business or international politics, but we can support and partner with folks who are called and equipped to do the macro analysis necessary for change at the national or international level.

But our individual choices also matter. Our lifestyle decisions reflect our Christian faithfulness and integrity as well as our commitment to the most vulnerable people. We can free up significant resources that can be invested in people, communities and ministries. With carefully thought through decisions, we can each have an impact on the well-being of hundreds of people living in desperate poverty.

John Wesley's model is helpful again. He and his coworkers were remarkably creative in sharing the gospel and in responding to poverty and injustice. They started schools for poor children and adults, orphanages, apprenticeship programs and medical dispensaries, and established loan funds for small businesses. The small group structure of the early Methodist communities made it much more likely that people from different social backgrounds would get to know each other and understand and address one another's circumstances. As people came to faith in Christ, they were nurtured toward maturity in a community environment that had high expectations and offered strong personal support.

Today we can make all sorts of decisions that show our tender hearts. Friends of mine (Christine) pastor a small country church in Kentucky that feeds several thousand orphans each day in Zimbabwe. They are able to do this because of how they have chosen to use their weekly offerings, and because of a friendship between a family from Zimbabwe and some Christian folks in Kentucky. As a congregation, they cannot bring about the needed political changes in a corrupt government, but they are able to make a difference in many lives every day.

After visiting with Sujana and her family again, I (Chris) decided to do something small and personal. I wanted to respond to the fact that millions of people live on less than a dollar a day by structuring my life in a way that helps me remember a few of those millions when I go shopping. I wanted to make the connection as specific and personal as I could.

I decided to implement a Personal Retail Equality Tax (call it my PRET). For the past couple of years, every time I shop at a store that purchases clothes from Sujana's factory or I buy clothing from one of the companies I know her factory serves, I tax myself an extra 12% of the price (it's just an arbitrary number, but it is a start) and contribute it to a PRET Justice Fund for Sujana's family. At the end of each year, we cash out the fund and deliver it to her family when we visit.

I'm hoping folks will join us in some variation of this plan. It represents more than sending a check to help Sujana and her sisters. It helps us make a direct connection between how we live, what we consume and what that consumption costs others. It's an awkward way to make sure a few people receive a livable wage—but it will make a difference for them and for us.

It's not hard to find fault with the logic of my particular approach. As one friend has already asked, "Taking your argument seriously, could people watch pornography as long as they taxed themselves and contributed to a shelter for abused women?" It is an important criticism. If we're taxing ourselves to appease guilt or to justify consumption patterns, we've missed the point. This is not an excuse to justify one's participation in unjust or evil structures. I can lobby Congress with Bread for the World or write a letter to a CEO each month to address structural issues. But in this case I want to do something to help my friends directly—friends whose wages are inadequate, and whose labor I benefit from.

For years, Mother Teresa was criticized for not taking on the causes of poverty as she addressed some of the symptoms. But the symptoms she cared for every day had names and faces and stories, and their particular lives and dying were better because she cared. It's not either-or. Global injustice and human need are so big that all sorts of responses are needed.

In fact, in my (Christine's) experience, holding together the personal and structural is the most powerful combination. People who offer hospitality to homeless folks or refugees provide very personal care and response. But most of them also work on the issues at a systemic level, otherwise the work is too small and too discouraging. On the other hand, doing advocacy without knowing any of the people for whom you advocate leads to a sterile and distanced kind of helping.

Sujana and her family really are poor, but they are not "symptoms" or collateral damage; they are friends. Bringing some tax money to them may not solve their problems, but if it can create a few new opportunities for them, it is worth the try.

Changing our spending habits so we can change our giving patterns can be a wonderful act of love and solidarity. Some might want to try a graduated tithe, determining what they need to live on and then giving away larger and larger percentages on each $1000.00 increment of income that remains.[16]

We can't get all "the plunder from the poor" out of our houses or our lives, but we can be more attentive to living justly. Are any of these responses sufficient? Of course not, but they suggest some of the many disciplines through which God could soften our hearts, change our affections and shift our attention.

Our friends don't have to be in India or Zimbabwe. They could be a lot closer to home. But we need to have eyes to see and hearts to feel the needs of those around us. We could start very locally with something as simple as remembering that if we have money to eat out, we should bring enough to tip the waiter or waitress well—so that their take-home pay at least gets to minimum wage. It's a small but effective way to make a significant difference in the lives of the "working" poor in our own communities.

Friendships with people who are poor or vulnerable can challenge our arrogance in thinking we know how to fix their circumstances. Our sweeping critiques of multinational corporations become more nuanced when friends are grateful for their jobs and proud of their products. Friendships undermine our tendency to locate the problem "out there" and to try to fix it at a distance. And friendship gives an urgency to our work for justice, to our search for ways to affect the decisions of multinationals and governments. Friends who are poor challenge our lifestyles of consumption when they build generous and gracious lives out of very few material resources.

When we get to know people who are vulnerable, we are challenged to take more seriously the power and opportunities we have. We might need to rethink our vocations in light of God's purposes for the world. Can we more consistently use our training and skills for human good? Can we use our leisure time in ways that more fully reflect our love for Jesus and his friends? Friendships with people who are poor make our lives bigger and invite us to enlarge our circle of responsibility. They remind us that our small lifestyle decisions matter—they matter to God, to our spiritual identities and to our friends.

3

Mutuality in Mission

*I*n Lima, Peru, the Word Made Flesh community works among a population of youth who are known to prostitute, smoke glue or inhale paint bags, and routinely commit crimes of petty theft. These young people live on the streets or in the slums of one of the city's most notorious neighborhoods. The WMF community lives and works there as well.

The first time Phileena and I (Chris) visited Peru, the founding field directors of WMF in Lima took us to a city park to meet with some of their new friends. At least three times on our way to the park with Adriana and Walter Forcatto, we were warned to stay out of that area. Our first warning came when we boarded a city bus and the Forcattos told the conductor where we wanted to get off. Without a moment's hesitation, the bus driver warned us *not* to get off at *that* stop—it was too dangerous.

When the bus stopped and we got off, we hadn't taken five steps before a middle-aged woman noticed that we were foreigners and discreetly cautioned us with a stern, though whispered, voice, "This is a very dangerous neighborhood. You should be careful."

Once we got to the park where the Forcattos had agreed to meet with some of the youth, we encountered a street vendor. She was carrying a large box filled with trinkets, gum and cigarettes. She stopped and asked if we wanted anything. We thanked her but said no, and she went off. After walking about fifteen feet past us, she stopped, turned around, and came back to warn us, "You should leave. You're not safe here." Then she went on her way.

In navigating certain parts of every city, one needs to use caution and prudence. The irony in this situation is that we were being warned about the very people we were going to meet. Locally, they call the children who live on the streets of Lima *piranhas,* the vicious little carnivorous fish that have been known to devour humans. The slur is meant to depict the way that the children rob their victims. Sometimes they gang up and surround a person, methodically picking through the pockets or purse of the frightened victim, and taking whatever they can find. In other cases, they surround a car stopped at a streetlight or intersection, breaking the window and reaching in to steal a purse on the passenger seat, or pulling a watch off the wrist of an unsuspecting driver.

The slang term is clearly derogatory, belittling and loaded with dehumanizing assumptions. And the assumptions are caricatures of the worst behavior, demonstrated by only a minority of the children who live and work on the streets. Nevertheless, all of the kids live under the stigma of the imagery.

Over the last fourteen years that the WMF community has served in Lima, staff members have earned the trust of these so-called *piranhas*. It hasn't been easy. It's meant being accessible and available to them, sharing cell phone numbers and home addresses. Such accessibility is risky, and many experienced folks in ministry warn against it. But the practice has allowed the kids to call on the WMF community at every hour of the day and night when they need to be taken to the hospital, bailed out of jail or rescued from situations of violence and abuse. It has meant that children have shown up on a WMF doorstep hungry, afraid, lonely or in need of a safe place to sleep.

Occasionally staff members have put themselves between a child living on the street and the swinging baton of a police officer, becoming a human shield against brutal violence. Walter Forcatto has been arrested three times in Lima for protecting children against police brutality, and once was battered himself while in custody.[1]

There are countless stories from the years spent building trust, cultivating relationships and trying to embody Jesus' love. On one sunny summer afternoon, WMF staff members met the kids in a city park to share food and play games with them. At one point in the day, some of the kids from the street noticed a couple of backpackers walking through the park. They immediately told us to go and warn the foreigners that they weren't in a safe neighborhood. Just who was warning whom? What makes us safe?

ANOTHER UNLIKELY WARNING

A couple of nights every week, the WMF community goes out to one of the red-light areas in this neighborhood of Lima. They generally arrive between 10 and 11 p.m. and stay until 2 or 3 a.m. Anywhere from 70 to 150 children make their way to the alley to spend time with staff members.

The kids range in age between four and their early twenties, and most of them show up cold and hungry. Many smoke dirty little cellophane bags of shoe glue or industrial paint to take the edge off their hard lives. Staff members bring something hot to drink and something good to eat to share with the kids. Usually someone brings a guitar and at some point plays a few worship songs, reflects on a passage of Scripture and prays with those who have gathered. Some of the children call it church.

One night, WMF staff members arrived at about the same time another group of Christians was leaving. They were from a well-known charity that sometimes visits with these same kids. When they come, they bring food and conduct a worship service with the children.

We were caught off guard when some of the kids warned us about the other Christian group. They explained to us how the group leveraged food for faith, and readily described the techniques the group used to get the Christian message across.

We hadn't really expected our young friends to be insightful and articulate about evangelistic methodology. But they translated back to us how they perceived Christian efforts in mission and created for us another layer of accountability. Allowing friends who live on the margins to inform us about how they experience some approaches to social ministry and mission helped us recognize what was off-center in our own work and when our attempts at love might come across as manipulative or misinformed. Their experiences of exploitation had heightened their sensitivity to inconsistency between message and method.

Rethinking Mission . . . Again

Friendship with people who live on the margins of the larger society, who are generally feared, excluded or overlooked, invites us to reconsider the meaning and practice of mission. Many of these folks dwell in what have been called the "burned-over districts" of "over-evangelized, under-Christianized" communities.[2] They have heard lots about Jesus, but haven't often seen him. When communities have been saturated with missional activity but the good news has not been embodied in a consistent presence of love and concern, folks know that they have been targets of one more program. And most of us resent being "targets," no matter how well intentioned the effort might be.

If we really believe that the good news at its heart is a story of God's love for us, then mission is being faithful in loving God back—being faithful to God, and to what, whom and how God loves. When our relationship with God is so compelling to us that we invite others to experience the same kind of life-giving relationship, we are in mission. The starting and ending point of mission is relationship, not only at the individual level but also at the level of communities.

When some experience, item, relationship or practice has brought us joy or healing, or when it has deeply resonated with our souls and imaginations, we often want to tell others about it. But outside of personal relationships, such sharing is often inappropriate. We don't generally walk up to strangers and share the details of our relationship with a spouse or even our favorite breakfast cereal, diet plan or music group. To do so marks us as odd, inappropriate, perhaps even slightly dangerous. What then makes us imagine that telling people about the God of the universe and Savior of the world outside of a relational context would be any less peculiar?

Important for our understanding of mission is the warning, often attributed to St. Francis, to preach the gospel at all times and to use words when necessary. It's not that words are insignificant or unnecessary, but when detached from relationship, they can be quite difficult to hear and comprehend. In situations where persons have been brutalized or have suffered at the hands of others, words of comfort, hope and promise—unaccompanied by presence and action—are small comfort indeed.

Most of us have come to faith in Christ through the loving example and friendship of others who lived well into their faith. If this is really the story of mission, then missional strategy and methods would benefit from closer scrutiny under the lens of friendship and fidelity.

The importance of friendship and mutual respect is not limited to ministry and mission among children who live on the street or other groups of vulnerable persons. I (Chris) recently had coffee with Beth, a good friend who directs an interfaith project. She is Jewish, and when we first met years ago she was immediately suspicious of me. After some time we formed a friendship and

Beth explained that she found it difficult to trust most evangelicals because of the tendency she'd seen on their part to try to subvert interfaith conversations and use them for apologetic or conversion purposes.

Our friendship has been mutually enriching and beneficial. As we drank our coffees and talked, Beth told me that she had recently made a donation to WMF. It is the first time she has ever given financial support to anything associated with Christianity. She mentioned that over the past few years, she had watched WMF closely and tracked the community's activities. The transparency and honesty she observed in WMF's approach to mission and in how it is presented in print and online made her respect and value the work enough to support it.

Beth knows WMF is a mission group, that it is organized around a common profession of faith in Christ, and that love for him is the motivation. But she also trusts us. Because of the mutuality discovered within friendship, she affirms that WMF is bearing witness to hope in a God who is good. Her relationship with Chris and WMF has not only invited her into a shared journey but has contributed to an accountability within WMF to make sure that love is the motive and framework for all of its activity.

CHALLENGING DONOR-RECIPIENT ROLES

Volunteering in Mother Teresa's House for the Dying changed my life. In my first two months in the home, I (Chris) attended to nearly fifty dead bodies. Young and old people, men and women, Hindus, Muslims, Sikhs and Christians—death did not discriminate.

During that summer and in the following years, I was privileged to sit with Mother Teresa around a dozen times before she died. In meetings with her, she would frequently say, "We need the poor more than the poor need us." That conviction has shaped the culture of the Missionaries of Charity who deliberately create opportunities for every volunteer arriving at the convent to minister alongside those who are poor and dying.

I was a college student when she first explained to me that I *needed* people who were poor in my life. Only after countless hours of working in the House for the Dying did I begin to understand what Mother Teresa meant. It challenged my assumptions about mission and my assumptions about who were donors and who were recipients.

Without the prophetic presence of friends who are poor in our serving and worshipping communities, how can we work out our salvation with fear and trembling, as we are instructed in Philippians 2:12? Friends are God's gifts to us, and without them we are incomplete; it is a little like trying to get a liberal arts education with only one or two fields of study in the curriculum. There's no way it can be complete—we'd be missing out on the wisdom and insight of entire traditions and disciplines.

But when we start fiddling with the notion that resources don't only flow in one direction, when we find grace and wisdom and gifts in persons who are poor and/or non-Christian, it is disorienting. It forces us to think a little more fully about the image of God in all humanity, about our own neediness and incompleteness, and about how God saves and transforms us.

WORKS OF MERCY AS A REAL MEANS OF GRACE

Recovering an important insight from the ancient church, John Wesley wrote that works of mercy are a real means of grace.[3] We tend to think that we draw closest to God in prayer and Scripture reading, in fasting or at communion. But works of mercy (such as feeding those who are hungry or visiting the sick and prisoners) are equally important as conduits of God's grace.

Because of some grave misunderstandings of the role of good works in Christian history—especially that we could earn our way to God's love and saving mercy if we just did enough of them— we've been hesitant to recognize that they are central to deepening experiences of grace and discipleship. Scripture does not detach good works from grace, and a fuller appreciation of the importance of good works in discipleship and holiness changes how we perceive their role.

If we see that care for persons in need is a response of love to Jesus (Matthew 25:31-46), a chance to walk on holy ground, then our entire understanding of mission and ministry shifts. It is not what "we" do for "them," but an opportunity for all of us to be enveloped in God's grace and mercy. In God's economy, it's less clear who is donor and who is recipient because all are blessed when needs are met and when individuals receive care.

FRIENDSHIP, DISCIPLESHIP AND COMMUNITY

One of the ongoing surprises in mission is experiencing how the gift of friendship contributes to discipleship. Many of the women and children with whom WMF works have suffered unspeakable trauma, abuse, violence and exploitation. And yet many continue to find the courage to pray. Their faith is resilient. They live with gratitude and hope. From their poverty they practice abundant generosity, giving freely and with joy.

We grow together in discipleship, learning from one another as we draw closer to Jesus. We do not bring the same experiences or the same resources into community, but through our friendships those experiences and resources can be shared, and they become the clay out of which faithful discipleship to Jesus is fashioned.

Mutuality does not come from everyone doing the same thing or making the same contributions. It comes from shared humility, respect and appreciation for the other person, and some sense of shared vision or purpose.

When I (Christine) worked with my church in refugee resettlement in New York, I became good friends with a young Cambodian woman who had escaped with her children and mother from Pol Pot's killing fields. Samneang had become a Christian in the refugee camps of Thailand but had begun calling out to "the Christian God" earlier during her escape. In the Thai camp, life was terribly difficult but a vibrant revival was going on, and many people came to faith in Christ. By the time Samneang arrived in New York City, her Christian faith was strong and contagious.

She and I participated in a small group that met in my apartment, and the members heard her stories of God's miraculous interventions in her escape and in saving people from death and terror in the camp. She challenged and inspired us with a bigger picture of God and wondered aloud why God seemed less active in the United

States. If we compared levels of trauma, loss and suffering, she was certainly the needy one, yet she brought life to the church community and to me even as we reached out to her and her family.

My church welcomed many refugees over the course of just a few years. As a congregation we matured through friendship with people from various, very different cultures. We learned the importance of fidelity and stability. A willingness to put down roots in a particular place and with a particular group of people provides a setting where over time we are forced to depend on God's grace as we work through interpersonal issues and go deeper into the Christian life. Such stability is a challenge to our contemporary tendencies toward self-serving notions of pilgrimage or journey that allow us to pick up and leave when things get difficult.

Sometimes we hesitate to reach out to strangers and people on the margins because we are afraid—there are too many unknowns. But as we saw in the earlier stories about Lima, safety and friendship are surprisingly linked—for everyone. In fact, friendship in the hard places invites a rethinking of what it means to be safe in any place.

When I (Christine) spent time with Catholic Worker folks in New York City, I was reminded of the close connection between security and relationships. As we walked toward one of the Catholic Worker houses, the woman I was with greeted by name a remarkable number of people. Almost all were folks that the other New Yorkers on the street were doing their best to avoid. I would have been nervous if I'd been alone. Over the years she had become friends with many of the homeless people in lower Manhattan, and while she asked them specifics about how they were doing, they also asked about her circumstances. There were many moments of obvious mutual affection that reflected a long and caring history of shared meals and experiences at the Catholic Worker communities.

Being in mission with people on the margins also reminds us of the importance of locating ourselves in places where we can respond to the initiative of another person for friendship. Unless our worlds are mutually accessible, all of the initiative is likely to come from one direction only. And unless a person has opportunities to offer friendship and gifts on his or her own turf, the relationship is unlikely to yield its most mature fruit.

The stories of friendships at the margins remind us of the power of hospitality and a hospitable presence. People are transformed when someone is willing to listen to their stories, to share a meal with them, to find their insights and concerns important or interesting. They are able to recover a measure of self-respect and a fuller sense of identity. But hospitality works both ways, and people on the margins also gain self-respect and recognize their own gifts when someone is willing to receive their hospitality.

Henri Nouwen has written that "we will never believe we have anything to give unless there is someone who is able to receive. Indeed, we discover our gifts in the eyes of the receiver."[4] Making sure that each person has a place in community and an opportunity to contribute is important for all of us.

THE IMPORTANCE OF EATING TOGETHER
One of the most powerful expressions of mutuality and friendship

is sharing a meal together. We tend to eat with people we like and with people who are like us. But shared meals break down social boundaries. All of us need to eat, and when we break bread together we embody our solidarity and common humanity.

Meals are also at the heart of the Christian story. Jesus frequently ate with his followers, adversaries and outcasts in the community. He was sometimes a guest and sometimes a host, but in either case, meals were important settings where he shared deep truths and insights about the kingdom, discipleship and God's priorities.

In Luke 14, Jesus is a guest in the home of a religious leader. During the meal, Jesus teaches about the banquet of the kingdom of God and how God will make room for people often considered unimportant or unworthy. Jesus tells the host—a Pharisee—that when he gives a party, he too should invite those he would usually overlook. He should make room for the people who don't seem to have much to offer. These folks, Jesus says, are the ones God wants to be included.

In this passage, Jesus invites us to think about the people with whom we share meals. He isn't saying that we should ignore our family and friends, but to make our circle larger. An important spiritual discipline around meals is to ask ourselves regularly, *With whom am I eating? Who is invited, and who is left out?* Our meals become kingdom meals especially when people who are usually overlooked find a place—a place of welcome and value.

In Luke 19, Jesus invites himself to dinner. He calls out from the middle of a crowd, "Zacchaeus, hurry and come down; for I must stay at your house today." Zacchaeus, literally up a tree, wasn't expecting any friendly attention—he was a despised and dishonest tax collector. How strange then that Jesus decides it is with Zacchaeus that he should have a meal. Jesus doesn't host Zacchaeus; he invites Zacchaeus to be the host.

To be willing to be someone's guest is an expression of respect for them, and many of the pious people of Jericho were shocked at Jesus' behavior. Out of the whole town of perfectly good people, Jesus—in their minds—clearly picked the wrong person with whom to eat. They knew it was an honor, and they were annoyed. But Zacchaeus, in his joy, offers to give away half his money and to give back four times as much as anything he has stolen. Jesus declares that Zacchaeus is a son of Abraham, this despised man belongs to God's beloved family, one of the lost has been found and restored. The meal gives us a picture of the kingdom being laid open by love. The kingdom of God is big enough and gracious enough to have room for the most unlikely folks and to give them places of honor.

In our shared meals, God is especially present. There is often abundance and an element of mystery. Meals are important times of healing and restoration and are central to most efforts at reconciliation. In the New Testament church, the early Christians struggled with eating together because of their ethnic and social differences. But they ate together regularly as an expression of the oneness they had found in Christ. Their behavior was so countercultural that the outside world noticed.

Jesus could have had us remember him and celebrate his love and sacrifice in any number of ways, but he chose a meal. His body, our bread; his blood, our drink. When our practices of communion or

Eucharist are closely connected to our common meals, we catch glimpses of the kingdom.

Years ago, I (Christine) was part of an amazingly multicultural church in New York. People from many nations worshipped together, but one of my favorite memories is of the meals we shared. When everyone brought a dish of food to share, we didn't necessarily know what we were eating, but it was a time when we drew closer in love and fidelity, laughter and gratitude, conversation and care. Most of the people in the church were refugees or involved in refugee resettlement, so it was a congregation that knew about tragedy, loss and displacement. But our meals together were a simple yet joyful proclamation of mutual hospitality, new beginnings and God's healing.

It's So Much More Than Food or Shelter

William Booth, cofounder of the Salvation Army in the nineteenth century, understood the central role of friendship in mission on the margins of society. Reflecting on his ministry with those who were desperately poor in the slums of England, he wrote:

> God, it was said in old time, setteth the desolate in families; but somehow, in our time, the desolate wander alone in the midst of a careless and unsympathizing world. "There is no one who cares for my soul. There is no creature loves me, and if I die no one will pity me," is surely one of the bitterest cries that can burst from a breaking heart. One of the secrets of the success of the Salvation Army is, that the friendless of the world find friends in it.[5]

Booth recognized that people needed friends in their journey to physical and spiritual wholeness. Ministry and mission at a distance can't mend broken hearts and spirits. He understood that if mission isn't connected to discipleship within community, most of the efforts go nowhere. None of us can grow into maturity without the help of others. The complicated ways that personal frailty and sin intersect with social circumstances make it very difficult for any of us to break free of destructive patterns without the support of a community.

When those who have come to faith are struggling with addictions or have been exploited, we can readily see that they need community or friendship in order to move forward in discipleship. But community and friendship are important to any evangelistic or missional outreach as well as to any church. Unless people who respond to the good news are folded into a community that is oriented toward growing in Christ, they are very unlikely to survive in a new identity, much less to thrive.

Friendship with vulnerable persons—especially orphaned children and widows, refugees and homeless people—reminds us that for Christians notions of friends and family blur together. We are both family and friends to Jesus and to one another. Jesus calls his followers friends, brothers, sisters and mothers. In Psalm 68:5-6, God is described as "father of orphans" and giver of homes and families to the desolate. In the New Testament letters, the church is referred to as the household of God (Ephesians 2:19), suggesting close familial relationships. This is not just an encouraging theological image for those without human families and social support;

it can be a life-giving reality. Offering one another a place to belong is central to what it means to be God's children and Jesus' brothers, sisters and friends.

SHARING OURSELVES AND OUR RESOURCES

In long-term friendships with people who are poor, we discover that friendship and possessions are awkwardly related. While social ministry is sometimes perceived as focused on helping people with their physical needs, friendship involves sharing ourselves as well as our resources. In fact, having too many possessions gets in the way of friendship because relationships are undermined if one person always has all the physical resources. Significant differences in resources can result in envy or paternalism, but when we share ourselves and not just our things, we become fruitful.[6]

Even when we are convinced that all that we have beyond what we need is not properly ours, we still need help in loosening our grasp on our things and in becoming more generous. *How much should we give? How much do we need?* We can't really answer these questions in the abstract or in isolation. But within the context of friendships that bridge large differences in economic resources, the answers become clearer. The needs of our friends become an invitation to practice generosity. Our own excess indicts us without anyone saying anything explicit.

Friendships also put pressure on our lifestyle choices because our possessions and consumption patterns are hard to hide from friends. That's why it is often easier to keep people who are poor at a distance—or to arrange to enter their world only through brief visits. Close proximity makes us more conscious of both abundance and lack. Friendships can move us to choose generosity over stinginess and modesty over extravagance.

Almost everything in the larger culture tells us that we've earned and deserve the excess we have. When we do share, it is usually out of our abundance. And yet Paul was able to commend the Macedonian churches because they shared "beyond their means" and counted it a privilege to help others in need (2 Corinthians 8:3-4). Viewing the church in Jerusalem as friends and kin, other churches gave generously and with joy.

There are few things less attractive than stingy Christians. We serve a generous, lavish God who delights in beauty and diversity, color and aromas. Choosing a simplified, modest lifestyle does not mean we are choosing boredom, monotone or continual penny-pinching. It does mean choosing creativity over extravagant waste and generosity over covetousness.

This is challenging terrain. But we can ask ourselves as we seek to change our orientation: *Could I invite my friends who are poor into my home and lifestyle and have a good time with them? Would I be ashamed of my comforts or expenditures? Is the embarrassment I feel an expression of my conflicted commitments and divided loyalties?*

LEARNING HOW TO BE HELPFUL

Friendship and mutuality have yielded additional insights. When I (Chris) became friends with Sujana's family in India, I was an ambitious idealist who had just recently graduated from college. I expected to be able to offer a plan to address their need and poverty. But the more I got to know them and the more time I spent with them, the more overwhelmed I became by their reality. Their circumstances were far beyond my problem-solving abilities. History, culture, religion and economic factors all contributed to the causes of their poverty and repression. I slowly came to terms with my inability to "help" them in any significant way.

But somehow coming to grips with my own incapacity to address their social and economic circumstances opened up the possibility for a very different kind of relationship. I needed them and their help. I didn't speak the local language, I was new in the neighborhood (and country), and I found it impossible to figure out simple things like going to the market or reading the local bus schedule on my own. They offered me very practical help.

Being far from home and family, the friendship they offered me was a gift. Our friendship grew as I took the posture of learner and listener. They welcomed Phileena and me whenever we returned to India. And over the years, we have brought many friends from the United States. with us to India, and Sujana and her family have welcomed each one with a cup of tea. They've stayed in touch through e-mail and always ask about their new friends in the United States by name.

Slowly over the years of relationship, we've been able to discern ways to begin sharing with them the resources and opportunities to which we have access. Because of several factors, including our friendships, the family has moved to a concrete home with running water and electricity. Devi, who played jacks with me when she was little, has been able to study at a local university. Sujana's family has done the major work in these transitions, and with the changes have come empowerment and freedom. Their lives have improved and we've been able to celebrate with them.

ANDREA AND VERONICA: A TREASURED FRIENDSHIP

Andrea Baker, WMF field director in Bolivia, describes the friendship she and Veronica have forged. Andrea writes,

> I met Veronica on Calle Carrasco, the booming red-light district of El Alto, Bolivia. In a desperate attempt to break away from the life she had known for almost 30 years, she was selling meals to the girls "working" the streets. Like so many of the women who prostitute, her story is one of abuse, betrayal, fear and survival, but Veronica has finally escaped. Over the years, she has changed from a quiet, hardened, self-protecting woman to a protective, faithful and caring friend. She's the jokester of our community, a hard worker who now knows and worships Jesus. She makes all of us laugh. She fills our drop-in center with beauty (flowers and plants in every corner imaginable), wisdom and strength.
>
> In the four years that I've known her, Veronica has become one of my most treasured friends. We share a love of gardening and worship. We're both feisty, sensitive and as hard on each other as we are on ourselves. Our arguments are often quite heated and then quickly resolved, usually ending in both of us needing to ask for and extend forgiveness.
>
> She was with me the day my infant son had his first of many terrifying seizures. She screamed in desperation for me as I struggled to resuscitate him. She lamented with me as

we watched his tiny body poked, prodded and covered with wires. And now we both celebrate his life. I love that Luke knows and loves his godmother. I love that she, in her own journey to healing, has allowed her heart to love a child, my child, without restraint.

Veronica's stories keep our community grounded; she gives us intimate glimpses into an underworld we're trying to understand. She cautions us when we're getting in too deep, and pushes us when we're tired and becoming hardened. She reminds us that our work is not a lost cause, not so much because she's a "success story," but because she tells us again and again how much it meant to her that we kept returning to the streets to visit week after week. Friendship with Veronica keeps me hopeful.

4

Naming the Ambiguities
and Tensions

*S*he said her name was Adalina and that she was sixteen. Her tender face and undeveloped body suggested she was most likely several years younger. She was shy and timid and about six months pregnant. Her heavy makeup and tight black shirt and jeans unsuccessfully masked her youth and made her seem even more vulnerable, sad and alone.

We were sitting on the sidewalk and getting to know her, but before our conversation got very far, the woman who pimped Adalina forced her to get back to work. Before Adalina left us, we tried to explain that smoking shoe glue was bad for her unborn baby. Our warnings seemed to have little impact.

I (Chris) have lost count of the number of times I've been sitting on a sidewalk in Lima, Peru, with a few children when a man two or three times their age walks up, takes one of the girls by the hand and then brings her into a nearby brothel. My anger boils, but alone I cannot do much. If I make a scene or intervene, I will make it worse for the children and youth who call that neighborhood home.

Word Made Flesh communities offer alternatives to prostitution and life on the streets. Staff members help youth move out of exploitative circumstances and move into a new way of life. But we also remain committed to the relationships we have formed with children and youth who for some reason are unable to break away or to take the steps necessary to change the trajectory of their lives. Sometimes the only way we can see and interact with these friends is when they are working. Being with them means being guests in their neighborhood, and being a "good" guest in a red-light area has turned out to be among our most challenging experiences, morally and spiritually.

No one imagines that being friends with these children in the midst of the corruption and degradation of their circumstances is a sufficient response. It is, however, a necessary one even as efforts are made to address unjust and illegal activities at a structural level. That child prostitution flourishes in some places is morally outrageous—it is obviously evil but it also reveals the underside of societies that many people would prefer remained hidden. After venturing into this miserable universe, it is hard not to respond to the most vulnerable ones, even when the responses are inadequate.

Where it is possible, we can partner with civil authorities and other agencies or organizations to shut down exploitative practices.

But often the civil authorities in the places we work cannot, or will not, intervene on behalf of our friends. So befriending people who are exploited—where they are—raises complicated issues. They are different issues from those encountered when we have more power or when we control the setting. When kids from the streets visit a WMF drop-in or community center, it is intended to be a safe place for them, and they are not allowed to bring drugs or weapons onto the premises. But when WMF staff members visit kids in their homes, on the streets or in the favelas, drugs are often present. In these settings, the dynamics of power and relationships are different. Visiting with young girls who are caught in the web of prostitution often requires spending time in the brothel areas. In a sense, the price of real friendship is that we go into this world disarmed of worldly power.

Our hope is that the children will get out, and that God will allow us to journey with them toward freedom and new lives. But sometimes it takes a long time, and often it involves fits and starts, moving forward, falling back and moving forward again.

Victims and/or Perpetrators?

When the line between victim and perpetrator is even more blurred, the questions raised by friendship become more painful and messy. During the civil war in Sierra Leone, a number of WMF staff members visited Freetown. At that time, nearly 60 percent of the country was controlled by the rebels, and the capital city was filled with internally displaced persons.

Driving through the congested streets of Freetown, we heard a public service announcement come over the radio. Bizarrely placed between a Tupac song and a hit from Destiny's Child, the government announcement demanded that the rebels lay down their weapons. It was a call to disarm.

At the time, the rebels had a reputation for being among the most cruel and ruthless people in the world. They were perpetrators of some of the worst atrocities in contemporary warfare. It was a terrible war.

We visited some of the camps for the wounded and spent time with victims who had been mutilated by the rebels. We became friends with some of the refugees, especially children who had been made orphans and were now responsible for their siblings. Many of the girls had babies of their own. Most of the pregnancies were the result of rape used as a weapon of war.

As we got to know the victims and to see firsthand the devastation that the rebels had caused, our anger and animosity toward those who had committed such awful acts grew more intense. It was simultaneously impossible to fathom and to escape the pain left in the wake of their utter disregard for human life.

On a rainy afternoon, we visited Waterloo, one of the largest camps for internally displaced people in Freetown. More than ten thousand people called this makeshift tent community their home. One of the residents was a boy named Madu.

When he was ten years old, Madu was abducted by the rebels and forced to take up arms as a soldier for the Revolutionary United Front rebel army. Trained in the jungle to shoot automatic weapons, he was told that he was fighting for free education for all children.

Madu, like many of the young children who had been abducted, was used in the front lines as the RUF attacked one village after another. He killed and mutilated along with the others.

We met him when he was fourteen. Still so young, he also seemed like an old man. He needed a cane to get around because his Achilles tendon had been torn by a piece of shrapnel during a government bombing.

Encountering the victims of the warfare had been challenging for us. Their stories were deeply distressing but their courage and determination to begin again was remarkable. Encountering those responsible for the terrible war crimes left us much more confused. We were unspeakably angry and sad. But we were also flooded with a frightening sort of compassion. Many of the perpetrators were young boys guilty of facilitating if not leading a war of terror—and yet also victims themselves. Simultaneously victim and perpetrator, Madu's story captured just how convoluted the practice of exploitation could become.

When Madu proudly showed us his fifth grade report card, we were the ones disarmed.

LITTLE MOVES AGAINST DESTRUCTIVENESS

It is hard to know how to respond constructively when evil and vulnerability, doing wrong and being wronged, are so intertwined.[1] If we keep our distance and stay away from the details, we can sometimes make the categories more airtight and mutually exclusive. But the stories of Adalina and Madu remind us that often it's all mixed up together. People are exploited and they exploit, they are misused and they misuse. Of course, there are people who are victims and others who exploit, but even then the stories are often messier and the histories more convoluted than they first appear.[2]

If forming friendships with exploited people is important to us, we will be drawn into some complicated situations. We will probably get splashed with some of the ambiguity and uncertainty. Can we really be friends of war criminals and girls who abuse their unborn children? What does it mean—for us, for them, for mission?

Ambiguities often cause us to pull away. The circumstances are too tainted, too unclear. We worry about becoming complicit in the evil, about facilitating the wrong or being personally corrupted. It's not just these very dramatic circumstances that challenge us—anyone who has a family member or close friend who struggles with an addiction knows about some of these questions.

We want to fix things and people. As Christians, we long to bring healing to broken circumstances and to be instruments of God's reconciling and healing work. Americans tend to take that a step further and expect to be able to solve problems quickly, on our terms and with our tools. But that assumes a level of power and control that is sometimes unavailable and often inappropriate.

In certain situations, choosing to be disarmed is the only way to be present. Without the power and resources that could substantially change the situation, we can still be friends. Jean Vanier has written powerfully about the importance of "accompaniment," being present to those with severe disabilities. Although their disability cannot be "fixed" or cured, we can each grow toward freedom and wholeness in community.[3] From his decades of experience in ministry with the most vulnerable people, Vanier concludes, "The poorer a person is, old or sick, with a severe mental handicap or close to death, the more the cry is solely for communion and for friendship. The more then the heart of the person who hears the cry, and responds to it, is awoken."[4]

When we allow ourselves to be disarmed, we become both vulnerable and strong. The only weapons then at our disposal are those of the Spirit. We choose the way of Jesus, laying aside all the earthly resources that give us power—in order to be present to those we love.

In Philippians 2, Paul challenges believers to love others with the same attitude we see in Jesus, "who, though he was in the form of God, did not regard equality with God as something to be exploited, but emptied himself" and took on human flesh. Jesus, in the words of an old hymn, "emptied himself of all but love."[5] Paul assures us that as we too choose the way of love and hold fast to the word of life, we will shine like "stars in the world," blameless in a crooked and perverse generation.

Choosing to be disarmed, as we are present to another person, is not the same as becoming complicit in the wrongdoing. If we ever get "used to" certain expressions of evil or the misuse of human beings, no matter how familiar the terrain has become, we are in trouble. The danger for those who work in the hardest places is that they might become calloused. After a while, the unthinkable becomes familiar and our souls wither. We become cynical and hard; the wounds that we have witnessed and borne become too much, and we allow them to become covered over with tough, dead skin.

We are in danger when we begin to think that we are alone in these situations. We are at risk when we forget that God desires healing, peace and justice and is at work in the world. As we continue to pray for God's mercies and as we faithfully offer a way out to people caught in exploitative circumstances, we give testimony to the power of love, forgiveness and reconciliation.

In his powerful discussion of reconciliation and being ambassadors for Christ (2 Corinthians 5–7), Paul warns the church not to be "mismatched with unbelievers. For what partnership is there between righteousness and lawlessness? Or what fellowship is there between light and darkness?" (6:14). In ambiguous settings, it is especially important to heed this warning and to distinguish between what draws us toward Christ and what pulls us away. Depending on their focus, close relationships can strengthen or undermine faithfulness and integrity.

In sorting out responses in compromised situations, we become deeply dependent on the community's practice of discernment. When brothel owners and pimps offer to rent rooms in their buildings to WMF so it can set up a clinic or social work office to help women forced to work in those neighborhoods, we need supernatural wisdom to discern the best response. In some situations this would provide the only care to which these women and children have access. Some are not allowed to leave the area, though WMF staff members can visit them. Even considering the possibility of raising mission support to pay for space rented from the very people that exploit our friends requires levels of truthful reflection and moral discernment unfamiliar to most of us.

Sometimes we can only do small things that reduce harm and give glimpses of the kingdom, trusting that if we are present in the midst of the difficulty, God will open up opportunities to minister and help. Such difficult choices humble us and force us to rely on God's grace and to seek God's wisdom.

LIVING WITH THE TENSIONS

When friendships on the margins draw us into morally ambiguous or troublesome circumstances, we desperately need to be located in a prayerful, truthful and loving community. We will not last in ministry in the hard places if we try to do it alone.

It's especially important to have practices of accountability in place that will challenge our tendencies to self-deception. Because we want to be good and we want to help others, sometimes we hide from ourselves what we are actually doing. We don't name the moral compromises; we overlook our complicity with evil or rationalize our failures. Deep humility, practices of confession and a willingness to speak truthfully into one another's lives will protect us from some of the dangers.

I (Christine) have mentored a number of seminary students who have found themselves working in these ambiguous settings. In our conversations, I've become more and more convinced that the ones who will be able to resist evil and offer hope are those who are morally and spiritually tender, deeply committed to holiness and integrity, and aware of their own frailty and dependence on Christ. If purity of heart and openness to the wisdom of others shapes every aspect of their lives, they are more likely to do well in complicated situations.

Ironically, local church congregations rarely offer the support and accountability needed by those who dwell or minister in the hard places. Most Christians want and expect success stories and clean categories. Missionaries and urban workers rarely find the freedom in church to talk about their deepest challenges or uncertainties.

In addition, a disturbing number of congregations make it clear that they don't really want people whose lives are a mess (especially after they've become Christians), who aren't cured of their problems quickly and completely, or who don't successfully escape troubled circumstances. Our limited patience is evident in how we hide from those with ongoing troubles, how we avoid people with chronic disabilities and those who are dying.

A woman returns again and again to an abusive relationship despite other options. A man, despite support, never seems to get fully past his addiction. These are familiar stories whose outcomes might eventually be good, but they are rarely resolved quickly. Stories from the margins remind us of the importance of faith-filled patience and trust.

When forced to deal with troubling complications, we often respond in one of two ways. We come up with a multitude of rules that tend to exclude troublesome people, or we become indulgent and give up trying to help people move toward maturity and wholeness. A longer, more truth-filled fidelity is needed.

Certainly we come up against limits in any form of ministry. Even if we are deeply committed to hospitality and friendship, we cannot permit friends or guests to abuse other guests we've welcomed or to undermine their chances at a better life. I (Christine) have a friend who teaches ethics at a seminary and also offers daily hospitality to homeless people, providing them with food and shelter and friendship. Through these friendships, his faith in Christ, daily worship and ethical reflection, especially on violence, have deepened. He recently had to exclude one of the guests from the community because he was selling drugs to the other guests. It was a necessary but difficult decision, painful because it was obvious that the drug dealer was also struggling, in need of friendship and in need of help.

Sometimes it is hard to tell whether our friendships have mattered to the other person. Occasionally, the folks with whom we form friendships just disappear from our lives. I (Christine) became friends with Carrie, a young woman whose life was a tangle of family problems and poor decisions. Although I felt like her older sister, I soon discovered that I was older than her mother, who had given birth to Carrie when she was a young teen. Carrie had two of her own children by the time she was seventeen. They were poor but she was hopeful, bright, funny and resourceful. We made progress on finding a vocational program and better housing. She came to church with me regularly and we shared several projects together and lots of meals. I enjoyed her children and her friendship.

Just as several promising options became available, Carrie dropped everything to return to her hometown and help her troubled and violent extended family get through another crisis. It seemed to me that she was throwing away a lot of good opportunities; for her it was a matter of responsibility to her mother and younger siblings. Carrie disappeared into her old life, leaving no address or contact information. I was sad and felt a little betrayed and very disappointed for her and her little girls.

I heard from Carrie recently—fifteen years later. She'd run into a mutual friend in ministry when she dropped her daughter off to begin college. The seeds that were sown years ago had sprouted; God had been faithful. And our friendship had mattered enough to her that when her daughter was able to achieve what Carrie had not, she wanted to share that joy with me.

WHAT'S AT STAKE IN THE EMPHASIS ON FRIENDSHIP?

At this point in our exploration of the gifts, ambiguities and complexities of friendships at the margins, some readers may have noticed that our understandings of friendship are different from some classical emphases. In the Christian tradition, friendship is often tied to love and charity.[6] In more classical or Aristotelian understandings, "friendship requires equality of power and status as well as shared activities, choices, and feelings."[7] In most of our stories, power and status are not equal in conventionally understood ways. But even in unequal situations, we have chosen to highlight the mutuality of friendship and the ways in which we help one another grow.

As noted earlier, in friendship, the other person is not seen as a project or needy recipient but as a fellow traveler. An emphasis on friendship in mission and ministry is closely related to cultivating mutual respect and valuing time spent together, not only because we are serving or helping the other person, but because all of us benefit. Friendship as a model for mission recognizes the importance of sharing ourselves and cultivating trust.

An emphasis on friendship is, in a sense, an effort to round out understandings of love that focus exclusively on self-giving and self-sacrifice. Love certainly involves sacrifice—lots of sacrifice—but it also involves deep relationships, mutual appreciation and communion. An emphasis on friendship is an effort to move us beyond duty-driven views of ministry.

TAKING FRIENDSHIP SERIOUSLY IN THE WORLD OF FUNDRAISING

The respect, mutuality, shared goals and commitment to helping persons grow that are important for friendship at the margins are important in every relationship. Whether friendship with a child who lives on the streets, a fellow staff member or a potential donor, the fundamental dimensions of friendship are the same.

When there are significant differences between persons in their status, power or access to resources, the possibilities of using the friendship for other purposes is heightened. If we desire the mutuality, trust and respect that are basic to the meaning of friendship, then we have to be very careful to resist seeing people primarily in terms of what they or we can offer or provide.

In 2008, WMF received more than 2.4 million dollars in donations. Much of it came in the form of small, regular gifts of $25 to $30. While occasionally the donation was larger, WMF has primarily opted for a grassroots funding base, cherishing the $10 contributions from children and seniors who wanted to help in the work. Not until after its fifteenth anniversary did WMF begin to relate to grant-making foundations. With little experience or natural aptitude for the culture of grant making, WMF's initial relationship to foundations was like a very awkward and unfamiliar dance.

I (Chris) remember a particular incident at an international meeting on mission and evangelism. While sharing lunch with some of the conference participants who were also our mentors and models, Myles, a new friend we had met at the meetings, pulled up a chair and joined us. He seemed genuinely interested in our ministry, but I was a little surprised as the questions quickly became more technical and focused. He inquired about outcomes, metrics and measurements for success and funding arrangements.

When we finished with lunch, Myles gave me his card and told me he was with a grant-making foundation. He explained that he would like to learn more about WMF and me, and to explore possibilities for a future relationship. He asked if I could visit the foundation offices.

I explained that everyone in WMF is required to find sponsors and fund their positions, and because Phileena and I live on missionary support, we bundle trips to save money. But I promised that as soon as I knew I would be in his area, I'd contact him so we could try to set up a visit. A couple of months after the international meeting, I got a call from Myles. After his warm greeting and some time catching up on news, he reminded me that he was still hoping I would come and meet with his staff. I explained again that I would have to schedule the visit to him along with at least one other stop.

Over the next couple of years, we infrequently exchanged friendly e-mails and Myles would call every four or five months. The script became predictable. I'd let him know that I hadn't forgotten and was sincerely looking forward to the eventual visit. It was probably the fourth or fifth time he called that the script changed a little. After the familiar start to the conversation and my promise that I'd be in touch when I knew I would be in his area, Myles asked, "Can I be honest with you?"

After my affirmative response, he explained, "I am doing my best to try to get to know WMF, but it's been very hard. I'm accustomed to ministries visiting us to fill us in on what they do. With WMF, though, I can't even get on your mailing list. I really recommend that if you want to raise money, you *make* time for people like me." Taken aback by what I was hearing, I pulled the phone away from my ear, looked at it and said, "What?"

That opened up a conversation that lasted over an hour. Myles informed me that each year, hundreds of organizations like WMF called, wrote and e-mailed his foundation. He explained that he'd never pursued a ministry so hard with such little success. All he wanted was to see if the foundation could support WMF and provide some fundraising advice. In retrospect, I can only marvel at Myles's interest and commitment to moving forward in the relationship.

I knew little about the foundation world's culture, but it was quite clear that our assumptions and expectations about donors and recipients had collided. Having seen some of the difficulties that friends in other nonprofits encountered in dealing with large donors, I was very wary. Programs and policies can be shifted in response to the donor's desires; the power that is located in the capacity to give a large gift to an organization is substantial. We did not want to be controlled or even pressured by people who we were not sure fully shared our perspectives and values. I also knew that the negotiations can be surprisingly dehumanizing for both parties, and we at WMF did not want to put ourselves in the position of conventional donor-recipient relationships.

As Myles and I continued our conversation, I explained that WMF sought consistency in all of our relationships. In the same way that we tried to resist the reduction of our friends on the street to targets or potential converts, we wanted to resist reducing our wealthy friends and acquaintances to potential donors. We were wary of relating to them only as a means to an end, of commodifying them as solely a resource for our work. Myles acknowledged the nobility of my ideals but replied, "Commodify me for a moment. I think we can help each other."

I tried to explain that cultivating a relationship with him was our starting point and more important to me than the support he might be able to offer to our community. I wanted to offer Myles a friendship with no strings attached because I knew that wealthy donors, grant officers and foundation heads could end up feeling personally used by a steady parade of people who wanted a handout. I didn't want to be yet another person who was more interested in how he could help us than I was in him as a friend.

I'm not sure the impulses were mutually exclusive, but it felt as if they were. The discussion heated up. In fact, it was passionate—two paradigms colliding, two friends trying to figure out how to relate to one another. By the end of that call, we were both worn out and needed a break. Myles told me that he'd call again the next day, but strongly urged me to talk to our community about finding a way to get me out to the foundation's office.

He called the following day and said that although the foundation had never offered this before, it had decided to fly me out to visit. I felt as if I was being invited to "audition" and reduced to a need his organization thought it could meet. I actually did go and visit him. It was a great time, the foundation's hospitality was wonderful, and our conversations were thought-provoking and intellectually challenging. We discussed organizational cultures, board theory and philosophies of ministry. I believe we were both enriched.

On the last day of my visit, Myles called me into his office. His entire staff was gathered in the room, and he described to them some of the more interesting aspects of the conversations he and I had shared. He highly commended the work of WMF and then said to me, "Our foundation would like to work with you to find a small $10,000 to $15,000 grant as a start. If we begin with a small amount, then our board will be able to track the grant and see WMF's effectiveness."

Again feeling reduced to a needy and immature supplicant, I was hurt and frustrated. I responded, "Or how about your foundation buys envelopes for our office for the next three years so you can prove to *us* that you won't try to control us with your gifts?"

Surely I could have found a more diplomatic way to respond. Not surprisingly, we didn't get a grant at that time, though Myles and I did continue our conversations.

After the visit our friendship started taking root. Maybe because we learned to "fight fair." Maybe because in "locking horns" (as Myles affectionately puts it), we learned we could trust each other. I grew to love him and have been happy to maintain our friendship. He has been faithful to me as well, and over the past couple of years, we've met up and shared a meal or two. Just last year he read an appeal in the WMF newsletter, was intrigued, and called me to ask how he could help. We spent several months working it out together. This time our interactions were reciprocal, mutually respectful and humanizing for both of us. It took time to build trust on both sides, but in the end we found a way to be friends and co-laborers despite differences in culture and resources.

Being on the receiving end of a person's or group's desire to help has taught me a lot. I was reminded of the importance of respect, humility and mutual vulnerability in long-term relationships.

CONNECTING FRIENDS WITH OTHER FRIENDS

Our friendship with Adalina has now spanned nearly ten years. She had just started prostituting when Phileena and I first met her; she was so young and naive then. A few years ago, we bumped into her on the streets of Lima. It was late and she was working, but we sat down and caught up on news quickly. She now has three young children who stay with her boyfriend in the slums while she works in the red-light area.

Because she needed to get back to work that night, she invited us to visit her home and family the following day. I was frustrated and sad. Our community offered her hope and opportunities. She didn't have to prostitute; we had people in the city who could help her. But for some reason, she opted for a life that represented real danger and deeply wounded her soul.

The next day we were joined by Sarah Dobrin, one of the WMF staff members in Peru. Together we traveled by bus nearly two hours to Adalina's shantytown on the outskirts of Lima. The living conditions in the neighborhood were terrible. She lived about halfway up a steep hill filled with narrow alleyways and hairpin turns. After following her through this complicated maze, we finally arrived and were greeted by her young boyfriend, who was shy and hospitable. He seemed embarrassed about his home and what his girlfriend had to do so that their children could eat. Her babies were adorable, but they were very sick, undernourished and afraid of us.

We sat outside in the sun on some wooden boxes because there wasn't enough room inside for all of us. It was a sweet time together, and despite Adalina's hardened exterior, we caught glimpses of the young girl we'd known years before. We laughed a lot. We got ice cream and soda—the kids loved it, but I think Adalina enjoyed the treat even more than her children did.

After a few hours they took us to their neighborhood park back down the hill. We followed the little winding pathways until they opened into a small area covered in rough gravel stones. There was only one piece of playground equipment, a slide. The ladder to the top of the slide had between twelve and fifteen rungs. Adalina's oldest child, along with a couple of her nieces, climbed up and down that ladder for close to an hour. The kids never actually got on the slide because the middle of the slide had been cut out and removed, leaving razor-sharp, exposed metal that would slash anyone who touched it. Someone had needed the material for their home, and the only equipment on the community playground had been destroyed to meet the need. It was a heartbreaking scene.

When all of us returned from the park, the kids were worn out and went to sleep. Adalina had an important question for us. She asked Phileena and me to be the godparents of her children. We were honored but also recognized the responsibility it would entail. We told her that we would need to think it over and that we'd let her know before we left Lima. During the rest of our stay in Lima, whenever we saw her (often while she was out working) she'd remind us of the request.

We really wanted to say yes. Being more involved in the lives of her kids might mean a better future for them. We wanted to be good friends to Adalina and to honor her as a mother. But really, there was no way we could have said yes. We see her so infrequently—we couldn't be present in the children's lives in a meaningful way. The permanent staff of WMF in Lima would be more accessible, but the years of friendship with us had built a special bond of trust.

We said no to Adalina's request. It was one of the hardest decisions I've ever made. We told her that we loved her and her family and that we would remain friends.

As we returned to our home in Omaha, Adalina kept breaking into my thoughts. I couldn't sit down at a meal without thinking about the hunger she and her children would be experiencing at that same time of day. Every time I saw friends' children playing outside, I thought of Adalina's babies and the sadness etched on their faces. Every time I saw a high school student, I was reminded of her lost childhood and inability to read or write.

Shortly after our visit with Adalina, I met a few folks as they passed through Omaha. They were internationally recognized worship leaders, in town for a concert. Over lunch, we listened to each other's stories and tried to find our way into one another's contexts. I had vaguely heard of a couple of these guys before, but as the meal progressed I began to understand the scope of their success and their impact on worship music. It was remarkable. I'd heard their songs sung in rural Uganda, South India and in the mountains of Bolivia. They were writing the songs the world was singing.

I told them about our recent visit with Adalina. Her story moved them deeply. Our conversation turned a significant corner when we began wondering together, *What kind of songs can child victims of human trafficking—kids forced to prostitute and former child soldiers—sing? What does worship sound like in their mouths? How do they proclaim the goodness of God when that goodness seems far removed from their experience?*

After working our way through more questions and laments, we wondered aloud, *Could we find the courage to sing the songs they'd write? Could we find new expressions of worship written by the victims of evil and exploitation?* Somehow Adalina was very much a part of the conversation.

After the concert, our conversation resumed. The worship leaders couldn't get the questions out of their heads. In fact, one mentioned that while he was ministering to the crowd that night, it was as if Adalina was standing right there. Somehow what he was sharing was for her. He told me that he'd take the memory of her story along with him throughout the rest of the tour. He wanted to do something specifically for Adalina.

Months later I received a letter from him. It was humble and honest, describing a commitment he had made to himself and to God that all the proceeds of the posters sold on that tour would be sent to Adalina. Tucked inside the envelope was a check for more than $19,000.

That's a lot of money for anyone, let alone for someone who has spent her life on the streets. I called my friend up and told him that we'd offer part of the money to Adalina, to help her get off the streets and back home with her family (over a hundred miles from the city), and to help enroll her children in school. I then asked if we could use the rest of the money to help the countless other young girls like Adalina working in the same red-light area. He agreed and thanked me for introducing friends to friends.

Adalina did go home and was reunited with her parents. But she still sometimes visits Lima. It has not been an easy road to freedom for her, even with help.

We couldn't say yes to Adalina's request that Phileena and I become godparents to her children. Partly because of the gifts of other friends, however, the changes in her life are hopeful, though incomplete. And Adalina, in sharing her trust and her story with us, has also changed us, our friends and our worship.

LEAVING FRIENDS AND TRUSTING GOD
One of the most difficult tensions in forming friendships on the margins comes when we have to leave our friends and cannot be sure they will be okay. Trusting God's care and sovereignty helps us

in these wrenching decisions. Being part of communities that will continue the relationships makes leaving bearable.

When it was time for Monica Klepac and her family to leave Galați, Romania, each goodbye was tinged with sadness. She had worked there with WMF for nine years and had formed many friendships. Her goodbyes with Ion and Victor were filled with grief because they were among the first boys she met who lived on the street. Over the years they'd visited together often, sometimes in the alleyways where they live, sometimes on a potholed handball court, playing soccer. They shared many meals—sandwiches on the street, hot soup at the drop-in center and pancakes at her house.

Both boys had lived with the Klepacs for a while, making the bond special. And each one had made an attempt to leave the life of the streets though both were ultimately pulled back to what was most familiar. Nevertheless, the friendships continued.

The farewell meeting was typical, Monica writes:

We had tried to tell the boys ahead of time to meet us for pizza at noon. One effect of years of drug abuse is memory loss, and the boys had forgotten our appointment. This was the last day we could come, so we rounded up the boys we could find. We are thankful that several boys have left the streets since we came in 2000. Some have returned to their families, some went to Italy, and some just stopped showing up. But Victor and Ion are still here, deeply entrenched in their habits and territory. Each leaves periodically to visit family, but they return to the shopkeepers and flower sellers that have become a surrogate family.

Today we found Victor in his usual position by the window of a shop, poised to beg from a customer. Ion was harder to find because he was literally locked in a shack. The boys received night shelter in exchange for guarding tools in a shack on a construction site. The one condition was that each night the boys would be locked in the shack from the outside by one of the flower sellers who held the key. Though it was noon, Ion was still asleep, and we banged repeatedly on the large metal doors to wake him. Victor ran to find the flower seller with the key while I went to a nearby pizza place to get lunch. Eventually Ion climbed up through a hole near the roof of the shack, walked to the edge and shimmied down a column to get down to us.

Our meal was simple—pizza with plenty of ketchup and soda. The boys laughed and yelled and recalled stories, but periodically they would stop their banter, and there would be a pause. Not a pause because there was nothing to say, but because there was so much to say. We all felt the pain of our upcoming separation. We took pictures and gave hugs and left them to the neighborhood they called home.

I am haunted by the image of Ion in his self-made prison. Locked each night in a dark shack, he also spends his days in an emotional dungeon. I pray for the release of my friends, but I have had to leave them.

We trust God that our efforts matter even when they are unfinished, because God continues to work through the community and within individuals. We are not indispensable, and we are not saviors. Nevertheless our decisions have consequences and sometimes they are costly for us and for our friends.

PURSUING JUSTICE AND CARING FOR FRIENDS

Friendships in the hard places expose us to the devastating personal consequences of evil and exploitation and give glimpses into the kind of help that is needed. Exploitation is a structural problem but it has individual impact. There is plenty of room for responses at multiple levels.

The issues of human trafficking and bonded labor became very personal to me (Chris) through Mansoor's experience. Mansoor has been a dear friend since my first days in South India (see chap. 1) when he, his brothers and his mother befriended me. He is the oldest of the brothers and put his education on hold to become the primary source of income for the family.

Life was difficult for them. They were part of a Muslim minority in a Hindu nation. They spoke Urdu in a Tamil region. Socially they were marginalized—a single-parent home was not looked upon well in their community. They were very, very poor; the brothers were just boys trying to provide for a family.

Gradually, the family incurred a tremendous amount of debt. Though he spent nearly every waking hour working multiple jobs, Mansoor still couldn't earn enough to make ends meet. As the oldest son, he took it upon himself to come up with a solution for the family's debt.

He applied for a high paying job in the Persian Gulf, spending months ironing out the details, securing the work permits and visas and then saving up enough money to buy a plane ticket to the United Arab Emirates.

The family was excited with him and for him. At that time in India, people dreamed about the opportunity to work abroad. What Mansoor would be able to earn in just one or two years seemed like a small fortune. With pride and hope for a better future, the family sent Mansoor off.

Shortly after arriving, Mansoor found himself trapped. Rather than the dream job he was promised, he found himself in bonded labor—a victim of human trafficking and modern slavery. Eventually Mansoor managed to send a fax to me detailing the tragic story of deception and exploitation. He pleaded for help. The letter was desperate; he did not think he could survive much longer.

We had to help. But how?

Buying the freedom of persons trafficked or sold into slavery comes with a bundle of ethical land mines. Goodhearted people and organizations are routinely criticized for purchasing the freedom of modern slaves because of the concern that this response perpetuates the problem.

Nevertheless, Phileena and I started contacting everyone who had been blessed by the hospitality of Mansoor's family over the years. All of them wanted to help and we gathered enough money for Mansoor to buy back his freedom. We did not do it directly; Mansoor was able to confront his captors and, with our help, buy back his own freedom. But he came home broken, humiliated and traumatized.

Being friends with actual victims of human trafficking makes our commitment to stopping it very personal. Our responses do not always line up perfectly with the most current social or policy analysis. There is sometimes a tension between what we must do in a particular and immediate situation for a friend and what we can do over the long term.

As a result of his terrible experience, Mansoor has become a more compassionate man. He was always concerned about those in need, but he is now passionate about helping to end human trafficking. His situation has challenged the WMF community to develop a fuller and more adequate response.

While we lament his experience, we are also grateful that Mansoor has been willing to share it with us. Through our friendship with him, our eyes have been opened to additional opportunities to partner with others in their journey toward freedom.

5

A Spirituality Fit for the Margins

*W*hat spiritual practices help us sustain friendships at the margins? What insights have emerged from our reflections in the previous chapters? What will help us stay faithful over a lifetime?

Despite its commitment to friendship at the margins, Word Made Flesh discovered that being closely involved in the lives of children who live on the street or who have AIDS and with women and girls enslaved in the sex trade takes its toll on staff members. Continued exposure to terrible atrocities and desperate need sometimes leads to deep weariness and burnout. The changes within WMF itself, from its beginnings with mostly young, single staff members to today with many more married couples with children, have also made it important to think about how individuals and families can flourish in mission over the long term.

These concerns led to the birth of the Community Care Center at WMF with its emphasis on spiritual formation, mental and emotional well-being and physical vitality. The Center provides tools for staff members to develop their own rhythms of service and renewal. Within each WMF community around the world, it has established the practice of "friendship mentoring." Periodically, paired staff members meet for coffee or lunch and ask one another: *What am I doing well in community? Where is improvement needed? How do my actions help community? How do my actions hurt community?* The discipline has provided space for fostering growth and for informal reflection on difficulties before they become major problems for the staff member or the community.

If we are committed to friendship at the margins, all of us need to ask what kind of spirituality will sustain us over the long haul. When we choose to dwell in places that have been devastated by human sin or exploitation, and when we develop friendships with people who are quite different from ourselves in terms of power, resources or life opportunities, what practices will help us maintain integrity and faithfulness? If we are persuaded that these friendships are what God desires from us, and that they are mutually helpful to us and our friends, what can we do to make sure that our friendships are more than occasional forays into another world? How can we resist an instrumental understanding of friendship that views our friends primarily in terms of what they offer us or our projects?

BECOMING FRIENDS OF GOD

The idea of being a friend of God should strike us as pretty outrageous. That members of God's obstinate, broken creation could be drawn into friendship with the Creator and Redeemer of the universe is extraordinary. And yet this is what God offers us. We are welcomed into the deepest fellowship and friendship of the Trinity. Jesus invites us in and wants to live in us. If this notion weren't so familiar to Christians, we might respond more often with grateful astonishment.

Jesus promises believers that he and the Father will make their home with those who love him and keep his word (John 14:23). He prays, "As you, Father, are in me and I am in you, may they also be in us, so that the world may believe that you have sent me." The possibility of mutual indwelling is overwhelming: "so that they may be one, as we are one, I in them and you in me, that they may become completely one, so that the world may know that you have sent me and have loved them even as you have loved me" (John 17:21-23). In these verses we catch a glimpse of an intimate community of love that turns outward for the sake of the world. Jesus closely connects our testimony and mission to our relationships of love and unity.

The scriptural story reminds us over and over again that we are loved by God. This truth tempers the temptation to think of friendship with God as something we have to earn. We do not need to work harder to gain God's favor or to be better so Jesus will like us more. Our belovedness—in spite of our sins and frailties—establishes the basis for a response of gratitude for the mercies we have received. Our lives then are offered back, out of gratitude, and with a heartfelt desire to love what God loves and live as Jesus' friends.

Most of us understand friendship with God in a very individualistic way—a close, loving relationship between Jesus and me. Such a relationship is a priceless treasure of the Christian life. Yet there is more; friendship with Jesus is also bigger and more spacious.

In drawing closer to Jesus, we discover that we cannot love him without loving others. Our friendship with Jesus does not become diluted as more people are included in God's heart of love. But neither can our friendship with him be overlooked because of others. The relationships are mutually reinforcing.

When we recognize the significance of Jesus' words in Matthew 25 that inasmuch as we have welcomed "the least of these" we have welcomed him, we begin to understand the extraordinary kind of identification and oneness available to us. As we love and live among those most likely to be overlooked—those who are poor, hungry, despised, imprisoned or sick—we find ourselves in intimate relationship with Jesus.

There is no way our friendship with Jesus can remain dynamic and close, however, unless we take time to be with him in worship and reflection. Little gasps for help or quick prayers of desperation in the midst of difficult circumstances do not sustain a friendship. In the same way that e-mail, text messaging or Twitter can only support friendships that are sustained by extended conversations and being periodically in one another's company, friendship with Jesus involves being in his presence, taking time to know him.

Our challenge, as we seek to draw closer to God's heart, is not to presume on the friendship or to take it for granted, but rather to cherish it. As we grow in friendship with Jesus, he will continue to transform our love to make it bigger and more fruitful. Love is not a scarce commodity we need to ration in case we run out. Friendship with the source of love guarantees that we will have sufficient supply.[1]

At the heart of mission is friendship. God's friendship is a gift available to anyone who is open to receiving it. It sustains us in mission as we introduce our friends to friendship with Jesus.

NOT PRIM BUT PURE

We live in response to and in light of God's friendship and goodness. What can we do except offer everything, our very selves, in response to God's mercy? Paul grasps this powerfully when he writes about offering ourselves as living sacrifices in response to the mercies of God (Romans 12:1). Living sacrifices—not dead animals, not substitutes, not giving something and holding the rest back, but giving it all in gratitude.

Paul gives us an idea of what such living and holy sacrifices might look like. He tells the early believers to stop conforming to the patterns of this world and instead to be transformed by the renewing of their minds. What patterns of the world got the early church at Rome in trouble? What threatens us? They, like us, struggled with pride and arrogance, with making inappropriate distinctions among persons, with envy and revenge, with returning evil for evil and with losing hope.

Our minds are renewed as we come to share the mind of Christ, as we see with his eyes and as we cherish what he loves. This renewed mind allows us to understand better God's good and perfect will. The change is radical. Our minds are not just altered—they are transformed.

This transformation is particularly important when we find ourselves working in situations of exploitation, injustice and dishonesty. The corruption around us can get into us. When we are surrounded by exploitative business practices or corrupt authorities, we sometimes conclude that for the sake of the kingdom, we'll do "whatever it takes" to improve the situation. But as we noted earlier, the means are closely connected to the ends, and despite the courageous ring to such a commitment, it is a very dangerous one. We cannot do "whatever it takes." In fact, we can never commit ourselves to whatever it takes. How we get to the goal is often as important as that we get there. If we do whatever it takes, our tools eventually become indistinguishable from the practices we thought we were resisting.

The way we take on evil and exploitation matters. With transformed minds and hearts, we do it with love and self-awareness, armed with the Spirit of Christ. We are tempted to take moral shortcuts all the time, especially when the situation is already complicated. For example, for the sake of a good cause or project, it is surprisingly easy to be dishonest with people who stand in the way.

Particularly when we dwell on the margins, when we are in circumstances where the line between victim and perpetrator is unclear, or where the distinction between ministry under difficult circumstances and complicity with evil is blurred, we desperately need a robust holiness. To live within some of these ambiguities requires a purity of heart that is not afraid of the tensions and difficulties and is not naïve about the human capacity for evil. Sometimes we confuse delicacy with holiness. Our protection is not in becoming prim, prudish or obsessed with rules. It is in cultivating a pure heart and the mind of Christ.

The holiness we need is simultaneously strong and tender. It is a holiness of heart that can experience genuine horror at evil, but also see human beings for what God intended them to be. It is a holiness that trusts God for redemption and therefore can sustain hope.

Such holiness is not there for the difficult places if it has not been cultivated as a way of life. How we think and act in regard to justice for people who are poor and exploited is surely part of holiness. But so is what we do with our leisure time and recreation. With what do we fill our minds when we have a chance to relax? The things we find humorous and entertaining matter to God and matter to the sorts of persons we are becoming. Sometimes there is a sizable gap between what we claim as our commitments and how we use our free time.

Paul's final words to his beloved friends in Philippi include an assurance that the peace of God would guard their hearts and minds in Christ Jesus. He writes, "Finally, beloved, whatever is true, whatever is honorable, whatever is just, whatever is pure, whatever is pleasing, whatever is commendable, if there is any excellence and if there is anything worthy of praise, think about these things" (Philippians 4:8). Paul was not saying to close our eyes to the misery, need or evil around us, or to create holy huddles that exclude, but rather, in the midst of the world, to fix our minds and to take our joy from what is good.

The holiness we need for living on the margins comes only as we draw closer to Christ, as we take hold of what he loves and cherishes and as we take on more of his heart and mind. The gracious surprise is that this transformation is not burdensome but a gift of freedom and grace and an opportunity to become part of the beauty of God's goodness.

Our holiness then is an eruption of God's goodness and beauty in the world. When we embody a unified commitment to personal righteousness and efforts at justice, we help to expand the possibilities of transformation and healing.

ROOTING OURSELVES IN COMMUNITY

It is hard to imagine sustaining significant friendships on the margins if we ourselves are not part of a community. It is simply too difficult to do alone. A community of friends who share our deepest commitments to God and to those on the margins keeps us accountable and gives us strength and support. But even more than that, it is hard to conceive of ourselves apart from the life of a community. We are who we are because of the communities in which we dwell.

No friendship with another human being meets all of our needs. Along with the blessings of having friends who are poor come some costs. Friendships with those who have been exploited can be challenging because they involve significant, even sacrificial, self-giving. In the midst of the rich mutuality of friendship that is available across differences, we also need folks whose friendships are easier because of our shared interests and backgrounds.

Unless our daily experience includes friendship with people who are poor or exploited, it is easy to romanticize those relationships. The reality requires honesty about the challenges and humility to recognize our limitations. The needs of our friends can overwhelm us, and ignoring our needs in those situations can result in very deformed identities and relationships. Multiple interlocking friendships within community can help all of us move toward wholeness.

Community is important for another reason. People who have been exploited need more than a single friendship. They need to be welcomed into a network of friendships and relationships where their presence and gifts matter to the community and where various members of the community can walk with them toward healing. Their transformation then becomes an invitation to the rest of us to recognize our areas of brokenness, further pressing us back to God's redemptive work in our lives and in the life of our community.

Attentiveness to the necessity of community helps us to see additional reasons for the inadequacy of career and cause approaches to mission on the margins. Unless we are involved in something like disaster relief as a profession, we don't usually make a career of befriending people on the margins. Friendship is part of a way of life, a practice that is relevant for whatever we are doing. Each of us is able to form friendships on the margins and to build community where we are, whatever our profession or calling.

Focusing on a cause can also allow us to overlook the importance of rooting ourselves in community. It takes deliberate work to link advocacy to actual persons for whom we are advocating. Cause-driven mission models can be quite individualistic. Despite the emotional high we get from bonding with others in working hard on a cause, we do not often form lasting communities with our coworkers or with those whose cause we are championing. A fundraiser that we do together to benefit victims of sex trafficking is not the same as creating a life together, living within the discipline of supporting, correcting and loving one another. Without such community it is difficult to stay with the concerns over a long period or to be transformed by those for whom we are advocates. While it is certainly possible to foster community within cause-driven efforts, it requires intentional effort.

CHOOSING GRACE-FILLED SIMPLICITY

Friendship with people who are poor often exposes our excess. This is especially the case if we move in and out of one another's worlds. We do not want to be guilt-ridden and anxious about our lifestyles, but we do want to move in the direction of justice and generosity. Getting a handle on simplicity that is full of grace is often challenging.

I (Chris) remember one incident well. I had just returned home from my time with the Missionaries of Charity in India. It was my first exposure to terrible poverty and death, and I was struggling to make sense of the disparities I encountered everywhere on my return. One of my younger brothers and I were playing *Mike Tyson's Punch Out!!* (maybe the best video game ever) on the original Nintendo system. As we played, my brother said, "Man, I'm starving. Want to get something to eat?" Given where I had spent the previous months, it set me off. I immediately thought of the corpses of the young men and women who had actually died of complications from being undernourished. So I promptly replied, "Dude, you don't know what it means to starve."

My brother, in an attempt to restate his original comment in a way he thought would be less offensive to me, tried again: "I haven't eaten all day, and I'm hungry." Still upset, I replied, "Well, how about I call a bunch of slum churches in India to start a prayer chain for you?"

It is not easy to move back and forth between different worlds, but I have had to learn that the grace and generosity I share with my friends on the margins is equally important for friends and relatives at home. Just because they aren't as regularly exposed to the tensions doesn't mean they deserve less respect or love. My lifestyle needs to be an invitation, not a bludgeon, that helps others to choose simplicity and generosity because it is appealing.

Friendships with people whose resources are very limited nudge us toward thinking differently about our own resources. When we love someone it is hard to hold on to what we have when we know it would meet a real need they face. Love, not guilt, frees us when friends become the prophetic presence of Christ in our lives.

Our possessions should not get in the way of our friendships, but often they do. They make us hesitant to open our lives to people who are not like us—either because friends have much less or sometimes because they have much more than we do. If we hold onto our possessions tightly or define ourselves by them, it costs us deeply in freedom and friendship. An understanding of possessions as given to us to use or give away allows us some individual flexibility with resources. All of us need to be careful of excess, and some of us, in order to live alongside those who have little, will choose a very simplified lifestyle. Others of us can use some of our resources to create spaces of healing and renewal—safe and good places to help those in our lives to flourish.

I (Christine) had thought that I would continue in ministry on the margins. After years of working in some hard places in New York City, I sensed God's call to seminary and further studies. I expected to go back to the city to minister, but when a position teaching at a seminary opened up, it seemed as if it was God's place for me. I landed in a small town, teaching at a large seminary, quite comfortable. I love my ministry with students and cherish the opportunity to train them for ministry, but I also fear losing the connections with people on the margins. Now I must make particular decisions to spend time on the margins. I need to think about friends who are poor in order to resist the lure of affluence and comfort or the dangerous notion that somehow my status warrants a certain lifestyle.

A wise friend once observed that we are most likely to worry about the people we see first thing in the morning. If we live in comfortable circumstances, we need to make decisions to plant one foot in another world. Only then will we keep friends in mind as we make our choices each day.

Real friendship involves movement in and out of one another's worlds, but our privilege, location and busyness often make us inaccessible to friendships with people outside our world. Sometimes we don't even see possible friends who, though not far away, are distanced from us by class or illness, status or capacity. Putting ourselves in places where people on the margins can find us involves slowing down, taking time to be where people can befriend us, and taking risks to be dependent on the kindness of strangers.

Within our own churches or congregations, there are often op-portunities for friendships that cross multiple boundaries if we would just notice them. We can also partner with others in min-istries that are built on and open into relationships, particularly relationships that can become long-term friendships.

GRATITUDE AND CELEBRATION

Without gratitude and celebration our lives shrivel up. While it would be inaccurate to suggest that people who are poor or have been exploited have a special handle on gratitude, it is a grace and practice often evident among people who are poor. Sharing life with those who are grateful for the most basic things in the midst of their ongoing difficulties challenges us and our more comfortable communities to reflect deeply on what we often take for granted— God's goodness and provision.

I (Christine) have a friend who works with homeless people in rural Ohio. Gratitude is a central aspect of their life together. During their "Friday Night Live" gatherings each week with home-less and formerly homeless folks, elderly neighbors and volunteers, there is always an opportunity to express thanksgiving publicly, and many participate. Thanks might be offered for a family member or for a good doctor's report or for victory in addiction. Sometimes it is for ketchup.

The director, Keith Wasserman, notes that gratitude is com-plexly related to service. It sustains our communities and minis-tries, but if we minister with the hope of being thanked or with the expectation that those who receive our help will be grateful, we will not be in a good position to respond when they are not. Life-giving ministry flows from lives that are full of gratitude to God, not with an expectation of gratitude from others. In community we can support one another, affirm contributions and yet also trust that our work is sustained by grace.

Gratitude often spills into celebration—for what God has done in our lives, for the gifts we have received and for the grace of friendships. Surprisingly, it is our friends who are poor who teach us the most about celebration. Those with very little often throw the best parties—sparing no expense. They find resourceful and often costly ways to practice generosity. The importance of celebration among people who are poor, or who have been misused, is a constant reminder that celebration belongs at the heart of discipleship and community.

Jean Vanier, who has spent close to fifty years living and ministering with people with severe disabilities, explains that celebrations—meals and parties—nourish us in surprising ways. To gather in celebration, he says, makes "present the goals of the community in symbolic form, and so brings hope and a new strength to take up again everyday life with more love. Celebration is a sign of the resurrection which gives us strength to carry the cross of each day."[2] Dietrich Bonhoeffer reminds us that when we share in something as simple as a meal, we have a mini Sabbath, a holiday in the midst of our work, a reminder of God's goodness.[3]

Our celebrations, whether simple meals or grand occasions, are communal experiences of joy and thanksgiving that renew us and give strength for the day. As Vanier has noted, a festive meal, shared in love, "is a sign of heaven. It symbolizes our deepest aspiration—an experience of total communion" and community.[4]

HOLDING ON TO HOPE

Sustaining friendships on the margins over time requires deep hope. Because transformation often happens slowly and unevenly, we can find it hard to be faithful and patient. In initial encounters with people who are in very degraded circumstances, it can be difficult to see past the misery and brokenness. Close to 250 years ago, John Wesley shared from his own experience:

> A poor wretch cries to me for an alms: I look and see him covered with dirt and rags. But through these I see one that has an immortal spirit, made to know and love and dwell with God to eternity: I honour him for his Creator's sake. I see through all these rags that he is purpled over with the blood of Christ. I love him for the sake of his Redeemer. The courtesy therefore which I feel and show toward him is a mixture of the honour and love which I bear to the offspring of God, the purchase of his Son's blood, and the candidate for immortality. This courtesy let us feel and show toward all.[5]

It was in part this capacity to see what God intended for each person—relationship, healing and immortality—that enabled Wesley to work for so many years among people who were poor and abused. God's profound, unfathomable love for every human being ascribes value and worth that transcends every human circumstance. When we recognize that worth in another person, it can yield a level of respect and mutual honoring that nurtures hope and fidelity.

We are also able to hold on to hope because we know that God's work for justice and reconciliation is ongoing and ultimately will prevail. Our present circumstances are not the final word, and a day will come when tears and sorrow are no more. This assurance is both a comfort in difficulty and an invitation to participate in God's present work of restoring and reconciling all things.

Those of us who live in fairly comfortable situations sometimes fail to grasp how important God's promises of final healing are to people caught in desperate circumstances. David Chronic, with WMF in Romania, describes his friendship with Marius, a young gang leader with clear leadership capacities who nevertheless struggled with the legacy of abuse and addiction. As he was drawn into the community, Marius grew in faith but continued to struggle. One summer he and his wife and children participated in a WMF camping trip in the mountains. It was his first vacation. David describes their conversations.

> One evening Marius and I sat outside talking and he started asking questions about things he was reading in the Bible. He didn't understand where God was leading him and his family. "We are poor and in need, but he is still with us. Still, we suffer and struggle with ourselves." I told him, "All that is true, but suffering and death are not the end of the story. God promises that there will be resurrection. . . . God promises to make all things new and that one day we will live in the heavenly city. The streets will be gold and before the throne

of God, gold will lose its worldly value. There will be light but no sun or moon because God will illuminate all. Sin, evil and the enemy of our souls will be no more, and we will bask in the glory of God" (see Revelation 21–22).

We talked some more, but then Marius asked, "Tell me again how it will be in heaven." So I told him basically the same thing again. The next day Marius came to me again. I could see the fire of hope and joy in his eyes. He asked, "Tell me again how it will be in heaven. When you describe it, I can almost see it."

Our times of conversation continued. One afternoon after the cooking and cleaning were done, Marius and I talked about some of the problems he faced. He asked me to remind him of God's dreams for his life—something that he loved to hear and felt proud to aspire to.

If we can be confident in God's good future, we can find ways to live faithfully in the present. The promise of a final healing does not displace our immediate efforts at justice, responsibility and reconciliation; it provides a way to move forward in hope in spite of terrible obstacles and disappointments.

Our hope is also sustained by people who become our friends and change our lives forever. Gautam Rai is a refugee from Bhutan. He and Silas West from WMF met nearly thirteen years ago on the streets of Kathmandu, Nepal. Gautam had opened a small momo stall in a closet-sized kitchen where he made and sold the traditional Tibetan dumplings.

Living in a tiny flat with hardly any amenities, Silas ate most of his meals on the street. Once he found Gautam's momo stall, he quickly became a regular, often having several meals there a day. Gautam and Silas slowly built a friendship; they ate together and talked about their lives, families and faith. Gautam, an animated storyteller, would recount stories from his childhood, his move to the city and the early days of his marriage.

He was married to Rekha, a woman from a village in the southern plains of Nepal. At that point they had two young children. The family was struggling just to get by, so at night they slept in the momo stand.

Gautam was interested in matters of faith. He was a Hindu, but when he was a child, his mother had been exposed to the Christian faith before she died. One day Gautam asked Silas if he was a Christian. Responding affirmatively, Silas asked how he knew. Gautam responded, "I saw you praying before you ate your momos. My mother used to pray like that." He continued, "If you ever have any spare time, I would like to know more about Jesus."

Dipa, the baby daughter of Gautam and Rekha, experienced occasional but violent seizures. During those frightening times, Rekha would grab Dipa and carry her up the mountain to Swayambhu, the monkey temple. There she would have a Hindu/animistic shaman perform a prayer to send away the spirit that caused Dipa's seizures.

Each episode was traumatic for the family. Silas asked Gautam if he could pray for them and for baby Dipa. Over the course of several months, Silas and the family became very close, eating most of their meals together. They continued sharing stories, and a deep and lasting trust was being established.

Dipa had another violent seizure. Once again, Rekha rushed Dipa to the temple, but this time the door to the shaman's room was locked tight. Deeply distressed, Rekha was certain the baby would die. Gautam wanted to give the Christian God he had been hearing about from Silas and the other WMF staff members a chance to heal Dipa. Against Rekha's tearful protests, he went home with their precious daughter.

Gautam laid the baby down and with Rekha's lipstick made a red symbol of the cross on Dipa's forehead as a substitute for the Hindu tika chalk mark. He placed a Bible he had received from WMF friends on Dipa's chest and stomach. He prayed a simple, humble prayer, and Dipa's seizure stopped. It was her last one, and Gautam became convinced that the Christian God was powerful.

When he told Silas the story, it opened up a very intimate exploration of faith, and Gautam soon asked how he could serve Christ. His life changed drastically, though Rekha still wasn't convinced. Her heart softened but she was deeply committed to Hinduism. The conversion of her husband created some division in their home. It took another two years before she made a decision to serve Christ and remove the Hindu idols from their household.

Since then, Rekha and Gautam have become pillars of hope and faith in the WMF community. They retired from the momo business and discovered a vocation in childcare. It started when they opened their home to children orphaned on the streets of Kathmandu. Moved by a profound sense of compassion, they took a few little girls into their home and cared for them as if they were family. It wasn't long before more and more children started coming.

Gautam and Rekha found ways to add more mattresses to a small and already overcrowded flat.

Silas reflects on the impact of the friendship on his life and on the ways it has given him hope in God's ongoing work. Gautam and Rekha and Silas and Kim and their families lived together for two and a half years. Through this shared experience of meals and living space, they established an intimacy that dismantled misperceptions that had previously limited mutual trust. They learned to confront and defer to one another. Mutual submission in decision-making meant that in later years, when Gautam and Rekha began assuming more and more responsibility, the leadership process was already established.

By living together they became far more than work associates or colaborers. Lives were interwoven through shared experiences and memories, late night conversations on the roof, babies born and raised together, caring for each other through malaria, dysentery, pregnancies and typhoid. Silas writes, "We could almost complete what the other person was saying. There was safety and trust in being so well known by others—and still loved and trusted in spite of it."

Today Gautam and Rekha run a wonderful children's home that feels like a big family. Gautam's wisdom and discernment continue to help the WMF community find its way through many difficult transitions and decisions. He and Rekha have remained faithful. Over the past thirteen years, they've welcomed nearly twenty WMF staff and fifty WMF interns into their lives in Kathmandu, while creating a stable home for the children under their care.

Rekha and Gautam, the Mustafa Syeds, Sujana's family, Samneang, Veronica, Adalina, Marius and so many others have invited us into their lives. We will never be the same. We have experienced the gift of mutuality in mission and our lives have been transformed. Friendships formed on the margins have formed us.

God's work of healing and reconciliation is mysterious, costly and wonderful. Being able to participate in it through the mutuality of friendship is a surprising and life-giving gift.

Journeying into places of suffering, abuse and abandonment takes its toll, but together with friends, we find a way forward, stumbling into the open arms of a loving God.

Epilogue

*D*uring her time living in the WMF community in Peru, Sarah Dobrin became friends with Adalina and many of the children who live on the streets of Lima. We close our little book with one of Sarah's poems. Zampoña, cajón, quena and charango are Peruvian instruments played by many of the children.

Out on the streets we say (the words ring loudly into my
    innermost being),
"Care for your bodies, spirits and minds . . ." and before we
    can finish,
A little boy speaks up with a grin,
"Because you are worth it, because you are God's beloved!"

The phrase bumps into the depths of my soul.
How do I begin to know?
Full of insecurities, fears and doubts.

Here we are, huddled close together.
And when we look up, we notice the Spirit of God
    embracing us.
With zampoña, cajón, quena and charango, shouts of
    laughter erupt.
The Kingdom is here, we humbly proclaim—
And then we gently lean up against each other.
Here we are, one with another.

Study Guide

Questions for Personal Reflection or Group Discussion

CHAPTER 1: THE VOCATION OF RELATIONSHIP

1. On page 26, Chris and Christine suggest that mission has sometimes been shaped by the assumption that "gifts flow in one direction only and that a substantial social distance between donors and recipients is necessary if not good." Where have you seen this assumption at work? What are the pitfalls? How does Word Made Flesh challenge this assumption?

2. Chris and Christine suggest that God wants to be friends with us. What does friendship with God look like? How is that similar or different from the way you think of your relationship with God?

3. Chris and Word Made Flesh use friendship as a model for mission. What characterizes their model of mission as friendship? How is this different from what you normally think of as mission? How does friendship challenge other models for mission?

4. On pages 34-35, Chris and Christine tell the story of how the disciples failed Jesus. They ask, "How do we measure success in the midst of ministry?" How does the story of Jesus challenge traditional ways of measuring success? What does it mean for faithfulness to be a measure of success?

5. Chris shares the story of being betrayed by friends at the pediatric care home in South Asia. When have you felt betrayed in trying to do God's work? How have you had to confront your own idealism? How do Chris and WMF respond to betrayal?

6. What is "travel voyeurism" (p. 39)? How have you participated in it? How does it violate friendship?

7. How does this chapter challenge you to think and act differently?

CHAPTER 2: RECONNECTING RIGHTEOUSNESS AND JUSTICE THROUGH FRIENDSHIPS

1. Chris and Christine suggest that we are bombarded each day with images and information that make us morally calloused. Can you identify anything in your life that might be contributing to moral callousness? In what ways have you been affected?

2. Chris and Christine wonder about how a sexualized shampoo commercial in the United States and child rape in Sri Lanka might be related. Do you see a connection between the two? How are our

personal lifestyle choices connected to global injustice?

3. How do Chris and Christine define righteousness and justice? How are the two related? Does your faith community focus more on personal holiness or social justice? What are the repercussions of your community's focus?

4. Reread Isaiah 3:14-15. How are you challenged by this text?

5. How can friendship with people on the margins reveal the connection between justice and our lifestyle choices? What does Chris learn from Sujana? How have relationships helped you see your complicity in injustice?

6. What do you think about Chris's "Personal Retail Equality Tax"? Would you consider joining him? What other personal practices might you consider after reading this chapter?

CHAPTER 3: MUTUALITY IN MISSION
1. In pursuing their friends, the Word Made Flesh community goes into areas that are considered dangerous, areas they are encouraged to avoid. What sorts of risks are required by friendship? Why do we resist taking those risks?

2. What do the children in Lima teach Chris about "evangelistic methodology"?

3. On pages 73-74 the authors write, "When some experience,

item, relationship or practice has brought us joy or healing, or when it has deeply resonated with our souls and imaginations, we often want to tell others about it. But outside of personal relationships, such sharing is often inappropriate." How have you experienced the truth of this statement? How does this statement challenge your understanding of mission?

4. How does "mission as friendship" challenge donor-recipient roles? Why does Mother Teresa say that Chris needs the poor more than the poor need Chris? ·

5. On page 79, Christine shares how seeing the friendships between a Catholic Worker and homeless folks in New York City reminded her of the importance of location. Why is location important? How are our friendships affected by our location? How does your location (where you live, work, go to school and worship) both limit and facilitate your friendships?

6. On page 81 Chris and Christine suggest that "an important spiritual discipline around meals is to ask ourselves regularly, *With whom am I eating? Who is invited, and who is left out?*" Take some time to answer those questions now.

7. How does having too many possessions get in the way of friendship? How might you need to change your lifestyle in order to pursue friendships with folks who are different from you?

8. What groups or individuals have you felt called to serve in the past or are you serving now? How is your relationship with those people "mutual"? How might your relationship with them become more like a friendship? What might be the challenges and benefits of such a shift?

CHAPTER 4: NAMING THE AMBIGUITIES AND TENSIONS

1. On page 96, Chris and Christine ask, "Can we really be friends with war criminals and girls who abuse their unborn children?" How would you answer that question? How do they answer it?

2. Chris describes friendship with Adalina and Madu as being "disarmed." What does he mean by that? How did he find himself without power in those relationships? Why is it both difficult and important to be present to someone whose circumstances can't easily be changed?

3. Friendship can "draw us into morally ambiguous or troublesome circumstances." What are some of the practices that help Word Made Flesh respond faithfully in the face of moral ambiguity?

4. Chris and Christine suggest that churches are not always able to accept ambiguity in mission. How does your church avoid moral ambiguity in mission and opt for easy success stories? How has your church been willing to enter into relationship with people on the margins? How might your church support missionaries or ministers committed to mission as friendship?

5. How does friendship as a model for mission affect fundraising decisions? What can we learn from the relationship between Chris and Myles? How would you describe the way each man understood the donor-recipient relationship? How do their worldviews differ? If you were in Chris' situation, how would you have responded to Myles?

6. On pages 91 and 108-12 Chris tells the story of Adalina. What is challenging about Adalina's story? What is hopeful?

7. In reading this chapter, where have you struggled or disagreed with the choices made by the authors? When have you faced moral ambiguity in your attempts to serve or befriend people at the margins? How might the reflections in this chapter affect your approach to mission in the future?

CHAPTER 5: A SPIRITUALITY FIT FOR THE MARGINS

1. How can we actively cherish our friendship with God? How are you already doing this? How could you enjoy your friendship with God more?

2. What is the connection between friendship with God and friendship with other people?

3. How do Chris and Christine describe the kind of holiness needed for engaging in friendship at the margins? When or in whom have you glimpsed this type of holiness?

4. Why is community necessary for forming holy friendships? What sorts of community or possibilities for community do you already have? What are you missing?

5. Christine writes, "We are most likely to worry about the people we see first thing in the morning. If we live in comfortable circumstances, we need to make decisions to plant one foot in another world. Only then will we keep friends in mind as we make our choices each day" (p. 130). Whom do you see first thing in the morning? How might you "plant one foot in another world"?

6. What is the role of celebration in mission? How does your church or community celebrate? How might your church's mission and celebrations become more closely connected?

7. Where are you in your journey with God right now? Are you burned out and needing sustenance? Are you feeling challenged, perhaps looking for a new paradigm? Are you energized, ready to begin new work? How will you move forward? How have your understandings of mission changed? What might be an action step for you or your community?

Acknowledgments

For their friendship and assistance in reviewing the manuscript, we are especially grateful to Rob O'Callaghan, Dave Chronic, Al Hsu, Ron Pohl, Jonathan Wilson-Hartgrove and Sarah Jobe.

Notes

Introduction

[1]Christine D. Pohl, *Making Room: Recovering Hospitality as a Christian Tradition* (Grand Rapids: Eerdmans, 1999).

Chapter 1: The Vocation of Relationship

[1]See, for example, Deuteronomy 10:18-19; 24:19-21; Job 5:15-16; Psalm 35:10; 68:5-6; Luke 4:18-19; 1 Corinthians 1:27-29; James 1:27; 2:5.

[2]Mortimer Arias, *Announcing the Reign of God: Evangelization and the Subversive Memory of Jesus* (Philadelphia: Fortress, 1984). In his book, Bishop Arias builds his argument around the deponent form *(euangelizomai)* of *euangelizo,* which essentially means the same thing but occurred more commonly in earlier Greek.

[3]Bishop Arias cites G. Kittel and G. Friedrich, eds., *Theological Dictionary of the New Testament* (Grand Rapids: Eerdmans, 1964), 2:706-25. See especially chapter 1, "The Good News of the Kingdom," in *Announcing the Reign of God.*

[4]Today Word Made Flesh maintains a "Vulnerable Persons Protection Policy" that requires signed permission and consent for any images of persons used in any of the WMF publications.

[5]Jackie Pullinger, Kingdom Conference Speaker, Asbury Theological Seminary, Wilmore, Kentucky, October 1993.

[6]Augustine, "Of the Morals of the Catholic Church," chapter 26 in Nicene and Post-Nicene Fathers, First Series, vol. 4, p. 99. Augustine writes on loving the neighbor as oneself: "Now you love yourself suitably when you love God better than yourself. What, then, you aim at in yourself you must aim at in your neighbor, namely, that he may love God with a perfect affection.

For you do not love him as yourself, unless you try to draw him to that good which you are yourself pursuing. For this is the one good which has room for all to pursue it along with thee."

Chapter 2: Reconnecting Righteousness and Justice Through Friendships

[1]See, for example, Deuteronomy 15:7-11; Proverbs 19:17; 22:9; 29:7; 31:8-9; Jeremiah 22:3; Matthew 23:23-24; 2 Corinthians 8:13-15; 1 John 3:16-18.

[2]See Stephen C. Mott, *Biblical Ethics and Social Change* (New York: Oxford University Press, 1982), esp. pp. 59-81.

[3]Gustavo Gutierrez, *A Theology of Liberation*, 15th Anniversary ed. (Maryknoll, N.Y.: Orbis, 1988), p. xxxviii.

[4]Arundhati Roy reminds us, "Being poor is not the same as being weak." See Arundhati Roy, *An Ordinary Person's Guide to Empire* (New Delhi, India: Viking/Penguin, 2005), p. 235.

[5]New International Version, Inclusive Language Edition.

[6]John Wesley, *The Works of John Wesley*, 3rd ed. (1872), Sage Digital Library (hereafter *JWW*), vol. 7, "On Dress," p. 34.

[7]*JWW,* vol. 2, "Journals," p. 351.

[8]In *JWW,* vol. 8, "An Earnest Appeal to Men of Reason and Religion," p. 47, Wesley writes: "If I leave behind me ten pounds (above my debts, and my books, or what may happen to be due on account of them), you and all mankind bear witness against me, that I lived and died a thief and a robber."

[9]Gerhard Ulhorn, *Christian Charity in the Ancient Church*, trans. Sophia Taylor (Edinburgh: T & T Clark, 1883), p. 303. See also the excellent essays in *Wealth and Poverty in the Early Church and Society*, ed. Susan R. Holman (Grand Rapids: Baker, 2008).

[10]*JWW,* vol. 7, "On Dress," pp. 33-34.

[11]See, for example, *JWW,* vol. 8, "A Farther Appeal to Men of Reason and Religion, Part II," pp. 215, 227, and vol. 11, "Thoughts Upon Slavery,"

p. 94. See also Christine D. Pohl, "Practicing Hospitality in the Face of 'Complicated Wickedness,'" *Wesleyan Theological Journal* (Spring 2007).

[12]*JWW*, vol. 8, "A Farther Appeal to Men of Reason and Religion, Part II," p. 215.

[13]*JWW*, vol. 7, "On Visiting the Sick," p. 141.

[14]In June of 2004 I bought it at $24.54 a share. Today (12/17/09) it's hovering around $21.77 a share.

[15]See Julie Clawson, *Everyday Justice: The Global Impact of Our Daily Choices* (Downers Grove, Ill.: InterVarsity Press, 2009), and Mae Elise Cannon, *Social Justice Handbook: Small Steps to a Better World* (Downers Grove, Ill.: InterVarsity Press, 2009), for more information on advocacy groups.

[16]See Ronald J. Sider, *Rich Christians in an Age of Hunger* (Nashville: Thomas Nelson, 2005), pp. 187-90 for a fuller explanation of how to implement a graduated tithe.

Chapter 3: Mutuality in Mission

[1]Walter Forcatto has been arrested two more times in Argentina where he now lives and works.

[2]John Perkins has said that we've "overevangelized the world too lightly." John Perkins, lecture, Duke Divinity School Center for Reconciliation, Teaching Communities Week, 2007.

[3]*JWW*, vol. 7, "On Visiting the Sick," p. 139.

[4]Henri Nouwen, *Reaching Out: The Three Movements of the Spiritual Life* (New York: Image Books, 1975), p. 87.

[5]William Booth, *In Darkest England* (Chicago: Charles H. Sergel, 1890), p. 271.

[6]See Philip Hallie, *Lest Innocent Blood Be Shed: The Story of Le Chambon and How Goodness Happened There* (New York: HarperPerennial, 1979, 1994), p. 72. Hallie distinguishes between giving things and giving oneself. He explains, "When you give somebody a thing without giving yourself, you degrade both parties by making the receiver utterly passive and by making yourself a benefactor. . . . But when you give yourself, nobody is degraded—in fact,

both parties are elevated by a shared joy. When you give yourself the things you are giving become . . . fertile. What you give creates new, vigorous life, instead of arrogance on the one hand and passivity on the other."

Chapter 4: Naming the Ambiguities and Tensions

[1]The title of this section, "Little Moves Against Destructiveness," is the way Philip Hallie described the work of the village of Le Chambon in rescuing Jews during the Holocaust. See *Lest Innocent Blood be Shed: The Story of Le Chambon and How Goodness Happened There* (New York: HarperPerennial, 1979, 1994), p. 85.

[2]See Miroslav Volf's work in *Exclusion and Embrace* (Nashville: Abingdon, 1996), and *The End of Memory* (Grand Rapids: Eerdmans, 2006).

[3]Jean Vanier, *Community and Growth* (New York: Paulist, 1989), p. 77.

[4]Ibid., pp. 97-98.

[5]Charles Wesley, "And Can It Be That I Should Gain." In *United Methodist Hymnal* (Nashville: United Methodist Publishing House, 1989).

[6]For helpful contemporary discussions on friendship, see Gilbert C. Meilaender, *Friendship: A Study in Theological Ethics* (Notre Dame, Ind.: University of Notre Dame Press, 1981), and Paul J. Wadell, *Becoming Friends: Worship, Justice and the Practice of Christian Friendship* (Grand Rapids: Brazos, 2002).

[7]Daniel Schwartz, *Aquinas on Friendship* (Oxford: Clarendon, 2007), p. 1.

Chapter 5: A Spirituality Fit for the Margins

[1]This reflection was drawn from "Spacious Intimacy: Making Room for God" by Christine Pohl in *The Cry: The Advocacy Journal of Word Made Flesh* 8, no. 1 (Spring 2002): 10-11.

[2]Jean Vanier, *Community and Growth* (New York: Paulist, 1989), p. 315.

[3]Dietrich Bonhoeffer, *Life Together* (San Francisco: HarperSanFrancisco, 1954), p. 68.

[4]Vanier, *Community and Growth*, p. 313.

[5]*JWW*, vol. 7, "On Pleasing All Men," p. 170.

About the Duke Divinity School
Center for Reconciliation

Our Mandate

Established in 2005, the center's mission flows from the apostle Paul's affirmation in 2 Corinthians 5 that "God was in Christ reconciling the world to himself," and that "the message of reconciliation has been entrusted to us."

In many ways and for many reasons, the Christian community has not taken up this challenge. In conflicts and divisions ranging from brokenness in families, abandoned neighborhoods, urban violence and ethnic division in the United States to genocide in Rwanda and Sudan, the church typically has mirrored society rather than offering a witness to it. In response, the center seeks to form and strengthen transformative Christian leadership for reconciliation.

Our Mission

Rooted in a Christian vision of God's mission, the Center for Reconciliation advances God's mission of reconciliation in a divided world by cultivating new leaders, communicating wisdom and hope, and connecting in outreach to strengthen leadership.

OUR PROGRAMS

- Serving U.S. leaders through an annual Summer Institute, gatherings, study weeks and workshops
- African Great Lakes Initiative serving leaders in Uganda, southern Sudan, eastern Congo, Rwanda, Burundi and Kenya
- Annual Teaching Communities Week featuring leading practitioners and theologians
- In-depth formation in the ministry of reconciliation through residential programs at Duke Divinity School
- Teaching Communities apprenticeships in exemplary communities of practice
- Resources for Reconciliation book series
- Visiting Practitioner Fellows

HOW YOU CAN PARTICIPATE

- *Pray for us and our work.*
- *Partner financially with the center.*
- *Join the journey.* Whether you are a student, pastor, practitioner, ministry leader or layperson, the center wants to support you in the journey of reconciliation. Explore our website and see how we might connect.
  <www.divinity.duke.edu/reconciliation>

Please contact us for more information about the program or to help support our work.

The Center for Reconciliation
Duke Divinity School
Box 90967
Durham, NC 27708
Phone: 919.660.3578
Email: reconciliation@div.duke.edu
Visit our website: <www.divinity.duke.edu/reconciliation>.

ABOUT RESOURCES FOR RECONCILIATION

Resources for Reconciliation pair leading theologians with on-the-ground practitioners to produce fresh literature to energize and sustain Christian life and mission in a broken and divided world. This series of brief books works in the intersection between theology and practice to help professionals, leaders and everyday Christians live as ambassadors of reconciliation.

Reconciling All Things
A Christian Vision for Justice, Peace and Healing
Emmanuel Katongole and Chris Rice

Living Gently in a Violent World
The Prophetic Witness of Weakness
Stanley Hauerwas and Jean Vanier

Welcoming Justice
God's Movement Toward Beloved Community
Charles Marsh and John M. Perkins

Friendship at the Margins
Discovering Mutuality in Service and Mission
Christopher L. Heuertz and Christine D. Pohl